Leading and Learning Together

Cultivating School Change From Within

Lynda Tredway, Matthew Militello,
and Joseph Flessa

Foreword by Mónica Byrne-Jiménez

TEACHERS COLLEGE PRESS
TEACHERS COLLEGE | COLUMBIA UNIVERSITY
NEW YORK AND LONDON

Published by Teachers College Press,® 1234 Amsterdam Avenue, New York, NY 10027

Front cover design by Holly Grundon / BHG Graphics.
Photo by SDI Productions / iStock by Getty Images.

Mouse icon by Fahad Hashmi from Noun Project (CC BY 3.0), https://thenounproject.com/icon/mouse-6945271.

Library of Congress Cataloging-in-Publication Data is available at loc.gov

ISBN 978-0-8077-8614-7 (paper)
ISBN 978-0-8077-8615-4 (hardcover)
ISBN 978-0-8077-8261-3 (ebook)

Printed on acid-free paper
Manufactured in the United States of America

Praise for *Leading and Learning Together*

"This book validates the deep knowledge and expertise of teachers, leaders, and all those connected to our schools. The heart of this work lies in *leading and learning together*–a collaborative spirit that unlocks the power of community to design schools centered on equity, belonging, and the boundless possibilities that lie within all learners."
—**LaShawn Routé Chatmon**, executive director, National Equity Project

"Through *Leading and Learning Together: Cultivating School Change From Within,* our educators have learned to use authentic classroom experiences as real-time student performance data. Their work with this text has resulted in a measurable impact on student learning and engagement. As researchers with meaningful experiences as classroom teachers, Lynda Tredway, Matthew Militello, and Joseph Flessa honor the complicated work of change, and offer clear strategies that will immediately resonate with teachers and school leaders."
—**Kelly McGuire,** superintendent, New York City Public Schools, District 2

"*Leading and Learning Together: Cultivating School Change From Within* presents a valuable new, yet ancient, way of knowing how be present 'in' the act of leadership. The authors reference the stories of hundreds of educational practitioners who participated in Community Learning Exchanges. Their struggle to 'breathe joy and justice into schools' is not easy, as it tests current paradigms while pushing new ways of seeing, being, and knowing. An analogy is like that of being on an elephant—you may first think that you are riding the elephant, but the elephant is carrying you. The authors challenge us to turn our practice inside-out, to embrace reciprocity, compassion, and joy through the activities they provide, which are more collaborative and powerfully unifying."
—**Maenette K. P. Ah Nee-Benham**, chancellor, University of Hawai'i, West O'ahu

"In *Leading and LearningTogether*, the authors help us reimagine what collective efficacy in action looks like as we continue the push for educational equity. They urge us to take an inquiry stance as we learn together in public and create brave spaces for deep and lasting change that disrupt the reproductive nature of inequity. In addition to giving us a clearer sense of the problem, they provide the tools and frameworks to facilitate change from within."
—**Zaretta Hammond**, educational consultant, author of *Culturally Responsive Teaching and the Brain*

"As a former superintendent of the fifth-largest district in the USA, I can say *Leading and Learning Together* is a must-read for every executive cabinet. The book reimagines educational change for school districts by sharing insight on reinvesting in the collective power of those closest to the issues—our educators. The authors provide invaluable guidance, backed by evidence from numerous school and district change efforts, making this book a practical resource for all educational leaders. This book stands out as a beacon of hope and practicality in an era where professional

development often falls short. It is an essential read for anyone committed to fostering meaningful and sustainable educational change in their respective school district."
—**Jesus F. Jara**, former superintendent, Clark Nevada County School District, and president, J. Jara Associates, LLC

"*Leading and Learning Together* is a must-read for educators, administrators, and policymakers committed to changing the traditional status quo of education. Based on 10 years of Community Learning Exchange experience at the local and national levels, the book's vision for educators to dive deep into learning from each other as research practitioners, use the community as a living text, and learn in public is integral to disrupting the 'grammar of schooling and hand raising,' leading to more equitable and effective educational outcomes."
—**Norman McDuffie**, principal, A. G. Cox Middle School, Greenville, NC

"*Leading and Learning Together* is a precious gift that Tredway, Militello, and Flessa have given everyone who is serious about equity-focused school improvement. Their extensive experience supporting leaders grounds the work of improving school in a realistic understanding of how messy and difficult it is and an optimistic understanding that together we can do much better for our young people. This book is a beautiful way for leaders to grow themselves while they develop engaging practices to lead authentic and democratic change. I cannot imagine a better, more thoughtful approach to supporting school leaders who are doing this hard and urgent work."
—**George Theoharis**, professor in educational leadership and elementary inclusive education, Syracuse University

"In *Leading and Learning Together: Cultivating School Change From Within,* the authors present a valuable resource for preparing educational leaders in a collaborative approach for addressing the complex challenges facing our educational systems. By emphasizing the power of unity and collective action, they champion a paradigm shift from top-down mandates to grassroots-driven change. Drawing on extensive evidence from their own experiences and the insights of seasoned practitioners, this book not only highlights the potential for educators to become practitioner-researchers but also provides practical strategies for transforming practices at every level of the education ecosystem."
—**Jill Alexa Perry**, professor of practice, University of Pittsburgh, and executive director, Carnegie Project on the Education Doctorate

"Your work has been powerful and influential in my leadership practices. The tools, protocols, and processes are a regular resource that I refer to when designing professional development, coaching leaders and teachers, and collaborating with other district leaders. It is easy to become a cog in the wheel in the world of school districts, but this book will keep me grounded in the moral imperative to lead justice-focused schools."
—**Janette Hernandez**, director of coaching and professional learning, San Francisco USD

Contents

Foreword

If I think back to my first memory of "being in circle," it was in my kindergarten classroom when I was five. In that circle, my knees touched the classmates to the left and right, my hands lay loosely in my lap, my eyes were fixed on the person speaking, and my entire body was still in attention. I can also remember the anticipation of when I would be able to share my thought or story or some other treasure brought just for this moment. In remembering now, I can identify that circle as a strategy to build and "hold" community, where all were included, all would have a moment to speak, and all were equal. There was—is—an eternal sense to that circle, as well, beginning everywhere and ending nowhere. That is the power of being in circle—not *a* circle or *the* circle, but of *being in circle*.

My ancestors knew it—most of the tables for large family gatherings in México and Perú were round; they still are. Indigenous communities all over the world know it. The circle is the embodiment of care, respect, transparency—it is the embodiment, the heart, of the community.

So why is it that we are hard-pressed to find circles in schools (beyond the early years—but even then, teachers often sit "above" students)? Why is it that despite many attempts at school reform, information, knowledge, and leadership are seen as unidirectional rather than multidirectional? Why is it that we are forced to distance ourselves from the circle and to think of our relationships and learning as linear and isolated? When did we become divorced from our ancestral and communal knowledges and humanity? And perhaps more importantly, how do we create, sustain, and welcome others into a circle of leadership—what the authors call "circular leadership"?

These important questions are explored here. The nuanced elements of how we learn, lead, and improve schools and districts *in* community, *with* community, and *for* community are at the center of the "circle" that is this book. In changing our practices to become those leaders we can embody that renewed purpose of schooling to foster and live in a socially just society. The authors do not promise easy solutions. They do promise that by following the practices shared here—from the inside out—we can all lead and learn in ways that help us reclaim who we are and who we are becoming.

My hope for you, reader, is that you will read the pages of this book and join this circle to rekindle your own memory of knees touching those to your right and left, allowing yourself to be still so you can listen intently, closing your eyes to widen your vision, and being unafraid to open your heart to the gifts offered by of those around you. I will happily join you there.

Mónica Byrne-Jiménez. EdD
Executive Director, UCEA

Appreciations

As with all appreciations, more people than we could ever thank are involved in a book project. First and foremost, we acknowledge the vital work of the practitioner-researchers—school and district leaders—who we accompanied and supported on their dissertation journeys and their participation in the microcredential as they enact their learning in current positions.

We are fortunate to continue working with our hermanos y hermanas in the Community Learning Exchange: Miguel Guajardo, Francisco Guajardo, Chris Janson, Kwesi Rollins, and Maenette Ahnee-Benham.

We acknowledge the work of the team involved in Project I^4, the federally funded research and implementation grant, in which we worked with school leaders across the country to use, improve, and document observation and conversation protocols. We particularly appreciate Larry Hodgkins, Carrie Morris, and Ken Simon.

Mónica Byrne-Jiménez, executive director of UCEA, has long supported our work in CLEs and as university-level practitioner-researchers. Her foreword reminds us that we must stay in community with each other. We have abundant resources that we can use to harness the commitment and resilience we need for change.

We appreciate our colleagues who graciously read the manuscript and endorsed the book: Maenette K. P. Ah Nee-Benham, LaShawn Routé Chatmon, Larry Cuban, Zaretta Hammond, Janette Hernandez, Jesus Jara, Diane Lau-Yee, Norman McDuffie, Kelly McGuire, Pedro Noguera, Jill Alexa Perry, and George Theoharis. We do this work together as compatriots who believe that public education is the backbone of a democracy and that racial and social justice is possible if we work collectively for change.

We deeply appreciate the ongoing support of Allison Scott as our editor.

We come from a long line of people who supported us at junctures in our careers, and we acknowledge the forefathers and foremothers of our work as teachers, leaders, and educational leaders who offered us guidance and opportunities. They inspire us to lead and learn with spirit, fortitude, vision, and compassion and create opportunities for others.

Introduction

The Circle's Web
Weren't we meant
To stand in circles
Feel the round
The curve
The energy inward
The momentum,
Next, across
The smiling eyes
Pick up the dangling word
Finish or help
Hold up, high five
Shoulder the sagging
Join hands
For grace
The glance of glee
The skip of laughter
The push of angst
The wave of mellow
Cradling the spell of memory.

Lynda Tredway, 1996

The cover image represents our commitment to collaboratively addressing school improvement and change efforts. The circle represents an ancient idea of working together to solve problems by fostering equitable and democratic leadership and underscoring collaboration and reciprocity. Circles are complex places where we lean on each other for support and often experience internal tensions and external demands. As Larry Cuban said in the book endorsement, "Changing schools is hardly a walk in the park."

Our intention in this book is to support leaders and teachers actively engaging with others to seek explanations and resolutions to complex dilemmas and challenges. We are stronger together. We have substantial evidence that educational leaders with teachers can become practitioner-researchers and transform practices in schools, districts, and communities.

Because school and district leaders, teachers, students, and families carry inside of them a hope of what could be, we urge educators to emphasize their knowledge, experiences, interests, and history in the schoolhouse and the district. Instead of a top-down, mandate-laden approach from outsiders—the systemsworld—we need to privilege insiders' stories, hopes, aspirations, and dreams—the lifeworld (Habermas, 1984; Sergiovanni, 2000). External and/or imposed solutions often impede the opportunity and possibility for authentic problem solving. We propose a different approach—working from *within*.

External pressures for schooling, while not new, are represented in a long history of grappling with the purpose of schooling—from the great equalizer (Mann, 1844) to liberation (DuBois, 1903; Woodson, 1933) to malleable efficient workers (Taylor, 1911) to a productive citizenry (National Commission on Excellence, 1983) to the emphasis on the economic purpose of schooling (Grubb & Lazerson, 2004) and the more promising attempts to engage in culturally responsive and culturally sustaining schooling (Battiste & Henderson, 2020; Gay, 2000; Love, 2019; Ladson-Billings, 2014; Paris & Alim, 2017). As we write this book, we are facing neoliberal practices that thwart the best attempts at equitable schooling for marginalized students (Helig et al., 2020; Schneider & Berkshire, 2020; Scott, 2016). While there is no one best outcome for education, we accentuate this purpose of schooling: *to foster, live, and thrive in a socially just society*. We take our lead from the lifeworlds (stories and lived experiences) of students and families by creating a gateway for equitable outcomes to redress the influence of the systemsworld (organizations and institutions). Easy to say, but more difficult to do—our experiences confirm that we can work from the inside out by leading and learning together. As a result, we can breathe joy and justice into schools and districts.

Despite the constraints of the current policy context, it's possible to collectively interrupt routine patterns of inequity. In the following chapters, we describe the necessary conditions to ensure a successful school experience: honoring the stories, experiences, and decisions of teachers, leaders, and families jointly responsible for educating children and youth. Any reader of this book knows that changing a school or district from within is hard for individuals, organizations, and institutions—all of which have calcified technical solutions to complex issues. Powerful forces impede innovation, rebounding to a hierarchical tendency and further exacerbating inequalities. Sanction-filled mandates may have laudable intentions, but, to date, they have not served our schools equitably (Levinson et al., 2022; McDonnell & Elmore, 1987; O'Day & Smith, 2016). While gross inequities persist after 20+ years of accountability and interventions, we suggest different ideas about marshaling the enormous resources of people and places in schools and districts so they do not get "stuck improving" as a way of being and can accomplish meaningful change (Irby, 2020).

We recognize that didactic and inequitable classroom practices endure despite substantial efforts to change (Cuban, 2023). The "grammar of schooling" metaphor describes the organizational and pedagogical forms of schooling that persist despite many reform attempts (Tyack & Cuban, 1997). As with grammar, the institutional actors follow rules and procedures, and predictable expectations guide performance and conformity. Any departure from the status quo may result in temporary changes but usually leads to institutional isomorphism—toward dynamic conservatism in teaching and leading (Darling-Hammond & Sykes, 1999; DiMaggio & Powell, 1991; Schön, 1973). Combining those commonly held expectations with policymakers' coercion, educational change becomes daunting, and solutions are short-lived.

In this book, we reclaim agency, advocacy, and inquiry for leaders and teachers in the places they know best—their schools and districts. Doing so requires imagination, cooperation, and transparency. School and district leaders as practitioner-researchers are well-situated to facilitate change efforts from within by disrupting and dismantling systems. However, justice-centered education requires the tenacity to use different processes. By concentrating on the assets of people and organizations to sustain lasting change, we share a set of alternative practices. By relying on the people who work in the schools and the districts, we can unleash the power of educators to work differently with school constituents and achieve more equitable academic, social-emotional, and civic goals. We intentionally use the term "constituents" to mean all persons who play active roles in the collective work of improving schools and districts.

OUR STORIES

We know the power of storytelling as a resource for connecting, learning, and working across boundaries of difference to achieve innovative solutions to seemingly intractable issues—like inequity. Through sharing our stories, we hope to engage you in telling your stories and connecting those stories to others in your contexts. Our stories are at the nexus of why we foster the work we do and have the beliefs we have, and they inform our daily work as educational professionals committed to social justice.

Lynda grew up on a farm in Nebraska, but, early on, began a journey to know and do beyond her dominant White experience—reading James Baldwin books from the public library and writing an American Legion speech in 1964 in which she questioned the Vietnam War and advocated for civil rights. Coming to Washington, DC, for college in 1966, she began teaching in 1969; as she often says, "I have stayed in the streets since then advocating for justice." She views her role as an educator as a critical space for supporting others to join the ranks of being and becoming antiracist leaders.

Matt is an immigrant son. His father (Ronald Angelo)—also his high school principal—was a second-generation Italian American who found his way to Mexico City on his spring break as a young public school teacher in Detroit. There, he met and married Blanca Rosa. At the age of 32, Matt's mom immigrated to the United States, and Ron's job soon took them to the rural upper peninsula of Michigan. There, Blanca, still learning English herself, brought her two sons to seasonal migrant farms in northern Wisconsin to teach English. This, combined with adults calling him "Taco," became his first lesson in equity. Matt began his teaching career in 1992—starting his journey to turn this equity lesson into his teaching and leadership practices of empathy and justice.

The explanation for why Joe dislikes talking about himself is likely found at the intersection of two core facts of his identity: He is both a person of enormous privilege (white, cis-gendered man with both U.S. and Canadian passports, a Berkeley PhD, and no visible disabilities) as well as a member of a small and often hated sexual minority. White men often take up way too much space, so he prefers to listen rather than talk; and, as a gay man from Ohio who got his start in education as a teacher of children in Texas in 1991, Joe knows better than to assume a friendly counterpart to any authentic self-introduction. An immigrant to Canada, Joe tries to apply the 5Rs he learned about from Anishinaabe colleague Jean Paul Restoule—respect, relevance, reciprocity, responsibility, and relationships—in his work as an educator.

Lived experiences matter. Understanding self so we can be in service to others is a shared tenet and drives our values as professionals. We began our professional journeys as teachers and still hold that identity as central to our work. Joe and Matt were school principals, and Lynda coordinated a teacher preparation residency program. We now work in university programs to prepare new leaders and support experienced leaders. As practitioners and researchers in educational leadership, we have experienced the merry-go-round of school improvement and observed the lackluster results of various school, district, state, and national initiatives. Based on our experiences with preparing school leaders—coaching new and veteran leaders, implementing strategic professional learning in microcredentials, and supervising EdD students and their dissertations, leaders with teachers can develop a collective culture as inquirers—in other words, as practitioner-researchers, they can collect and analyze available daily evidence from their schools. By using evidence and working in collaboration with one another, school and district leaders can engage in the teaching and learning practices our students, families, and communities need and deserve.

LEADING AND LEARNING TOGETHER

The changes we propose might be more accurately termed a resurgence of what is well-known about learning theory, neuroscience, dialogical learning, equitable access for adult and student learning, participatory action and activist research practices, and Indigenous ways of knowing, being, and acting (Benham & Cooper, 2000; Benham & Napier, 2002; Hammond, 2015; hunter et al., 2013; Mitchell, 2018; National Academy of Sciences, 2018; Roberts, 2023). The lifeworld of the people who work in schools and districts—their lived experiences and values—can act as a humanizing force that informs and supports the systemsworld rather than the system controlling the people. Their stories, experiences, and cultural values should inform the school community and become the text we use for change (see Chapter 3). We offer evidence of how organizational actors—school and district leaders with teachers—can learn to be participatory action and activist researchers. As critical inquirers of their work, they should be the primary decision-makers about change efforts (Kemmis et al., 2014). School and district goals would be better served by examining collective assets to address challenges and using qualitative research processes to instill a culture of participatory action and activist research. School leaders must assume their rightful and righteous role as practitioner-researchers to cultivate change from within.

We offer flexible and contextualized processes anchored in social justice to guide the educational reform we have yet to fully achieve. We deconstruct the grammar of schooling to realize democratic education ideals (Dewey, 1916) and proffer these considerations to embrace *leading and learning together*:

1. *The Leadership Pivot*
    - Leadership as a function in schools and districts that questions the single or hero leader (Benham & Napier, 2002; Kim & Mauldlin, 2022; Spillane et al., 2001)
    - Social justice leaders as equity warriors and co-conspirators who balance beliefs with practices to ensure equitable academic and social-emotional educational experiences and student outcomes (Leverett, 2002; Love, 2019; Mitchell, 2018)
    - The transparency and vulnerability to learn in public with one another by sustaining gracious space (Hughes & Grace, 2011)
2. *The Pedagogy of Trust*
    - Commitment to personal development that includes self-awareness and understanding of racial, cultural, and gender identity of self and others (Drago-Severson et al., 2023; Gooden & O'Doherty, 2015; Hammond, 2015; Khalifa, 2018)
    - Building and sustaining trust over time by privileging our lifeworld as an intrinsic and essential process of reforming schools and organizations—the systemsworld (Bryk et al., 2010; Sergiovanni, 2000; Tredway et al., 2020)
3. *Community as Text*
    - Contextual power of place and wisdom of people as assets to empower groups of people to address local issues (Guajardo et al., 2016)
    - Collectively diagnosing and co-designing responses to local issues (Spillane, 2013)

School and district leaders must simultaneously facilitate change processes and be ready to let go of the convening and facilitation functions as others become adept at the processes we propose. We make better decisions by focusing on assets, including the potential for collaborative leadership, and using equity as a guiding light. When leaders and teachers collectively use evidence to engage in praxis—deep, critical reflection that informs actions (Freire, 1970), they make informed, collaborative, and evidence-based decisions.

Our work with leaders indicates that *leading and learning together* requires a foundation of purposefully and relentlessly building a pedagogy of relational trust. By working from the inside out, we can bend the arc of social justice practice toward equitable access and rigor (Grubb & Tredway, 2010; Boykin & Noguera, 2011). School and district leaders are critical linchpins for fully engaging teachers, parents, and students to promote equitable and durable academic, social-emotional, and civic student outcomes. Effective leaders facilitating groups of committed educators can gather evidence to support decisions about professional learning and co-develop their learning with an equity lens in mind as they focus on what *leadership and learning together* look like in theory and practice. We stand at the ready to support leaders as equity warriors who accept challenges and guide others while learning how and when to lead and when to step aside and let others lead (Militello & Morris, 2023; Mitchell, 2018; Leverett, 2002).

STRUCTURE OF THE BOOK

The book is for practitioners—school and district leaders and teachers—who want to reimagine their work. The book is also for leadership faculty who prepare and support them. We urge readers to claim the practitioner-researcher role as they facilitate learning for others. Because school and district change requires a personal and professional commitment, we pepper the book with stories—ours and those of others with whom we have worked—creating brave spaces for dialogue and using storytelling are binding ingredients of school change (Machado, 2021; Quadros-Meis, 2021). In addition, our suggestions result from an analysis of EdD participatory action and activist dissertation studies, school leaders who participated in professional learning experiences, and our research efforts. In every chapter, we offer tools and resources to support readers in changing their practices. In Part I, we center on the capacity to cultivate change. In Part II, we offer examples of change in action. The protocols we describe are accessible at https://www.tcpress.com/filebin/PDFs/9780807786147_supp.pdf.

Part I: The Capacity We Need to Cultivate Change

We support a leadership model that combines the elements of joint enterprise, mutual engagement, and shared repertoire (Spillane, 2006; Wenger, 1998). The people in schools and districts form the critical infrastructure that can interrupt the grammar of schooling and establish and maintain the necessary conditions for school and district change efforts.

- In Chapter 1, *The Leadership Pivot: From Single to Many*, we highlight how collective work in education is a cornerstone of democracy and ensures access and improved outcomes for our most vulnerable citizens.
- In Chapter 2, *The Pedagogy of Trust: Setting the Necessary Conditions*, we magnify how to breathe joy and justice into schools, districts, and communities.
- In Chapter 3, *Community as Text: Harnessing the Assets of People and Place*, we use the "text" that arises from Community Learning Exchange (CLE) axioms, gracious space principles, and participatory and dialogical practices as noncanonical ways of being, knowing, and doing.

Part II: Changes in Practice

In Part II, we highlight the procedural "how" and subscribe to building capacity from the inside out, by providing examples of how educational practitioners integrate the pedagogical and research theory described in Part I with stories and lessons of transfer.

- In Chapter 4, *Practitioner-Research in Action*, we assert how leaders and teachers can become participatory action and activist researchers by using evidence to make decisions.
- In Chapter 5, *Evidence-Based Observations*, and Chapter 6, *Effective Conversations, Not Feedback*, we describe how school leaders with teachers or district supervisors with principals use evidence-based observations to collect and analyze classroom data and have productive conversations.
- In Chapter 7, *Authentic and Meaningful Professional Learning*, we examine how the people closest to the work should "take back" responsibility for professional learning. Professional development is not an event but professionals' daily work in conversation about their practices.

We conclude with a final chapter centered on *Leading and Learning With Joy and Justice.* With online tools and resources accessible via QR Code (see gray box below), the reader has immediate access to the processes that support the immediate application of *leading and learning together*.

We hope to excite all readers to become practitioner-researchers and reignite your passion for why you do this work. We invite you to use the protocols but insist that you contextualize and modify processes to meet the needs of your communities. Our ultimate aim is to provide strategies to liberate leadership from a solo, often lonely, act to actions as practitioner-researchers who harness the wisdom of people and the power of place. A circle's web can either entangle or support. When leading and learning with others, our authentic and genuine processes offer a path to justice. When leading and learning is reciprocal, our experiences and evidence reify the poem's line "*weren't we meant to stand in circles?*"

ONLINE RESOURCES

https://www.tcpress.com/filebin/PDFs/9780807786147supp.pdf

Part I

THE CAPACITY WE NEED TO CULTIVATE CHANGE

CHAPTER 1

The Leadership Pivot

From Single to Many

> With the principal-centered school model, leaders can easily reinforce "power over" approaches to teachers, parents, and families, by positioning principals as a central source of leadership thus neglecting the critical insights and vantage points these communities bring.
>
> (Kim & Mauldin, 2022, p. 10)

To accomplish the goals of schooling and shift leadership practices in schools and districts from single to many—from leadership as a person to leadership as a function, we offer a mashup—a creative concept in which we blend or mashup different sources or genres as a resource for understanding the multiple disciplinary approaches to leadership. In a music mashup, artists make innovative pieces by mixing the vocals of one song with instrumental tracks from another. In our mashup, we consider multiple viewpoints and canons, blending the old and new to cultivate the incremental and systemic change necessary to shift practices. In discussing the disciplinary approaches that inform and often confound leadership, we mesh practices with what we know about knowing, learning, and doing to contrast hierarchical with circular leadership. In shifting how leaders come to know and act, we blend teaching and learning knowledge with culturally responsive pedagogy. We conclude the chapter with a discussion of social justice leadership.

DISCIPLINARY APPROACHES TO LEADERSHIP

Reformers use multiple disciplinary perspectives to inform leaders and teachers about what and how to change. Yet, too often, change efforts are not guided from the inside out but from the outside in. We offer an alternative—shifting leadership to *leading and learning* together. To resist current policies and practices that privilege the outside-in approach, we take a different stance—shifting from hierarchical leadership to providing and including an inside-out approach that includes other constituents. Because the institutional (systemsworld) overwhelms most progress in schools (Weiss, 1995), organizational actors typically fall in line with the hierarchy. We believe school and district leaders are uniquely situated to resist this pressure when they view and enact leadership as a function in schools (Spillane et al., 2001). When leaders respect, identify, and work with teachers, they can use their collective knowledge and skills to make change. In Table 1.1, we summarize the driving questions for multiple disciplines and the leadership responses in institutions and organizations necessary for enacting *leading and learning.*

Table 1.1. Disciplinary Approaches and Questions for Leading and Learning

Discipline	Driving Questions	Leading and Learning Responses
Economics	Who gets what, when, and how? What drives decisions to allocate resources?	Redefine incentives, efficiency, and costs/benefits to promote equitable allocation and outcomes.
Sociology	How do groups of people conform? Who gets left out? What norms and routines do or do not promote equitable participation and outcomes?	Engage and honor all voices by ensuring the participation and ideas of historically marginalized groups.
Physiology	How does the brain react and evolve to understand and accept change? How do we promote self-care as a basic tenet of enacting social justice?	Reorient systems to address perpetual traumatic stress from oppression and institute self-care as a ritual in organizational systems.
Psychology	How do individuals accommodate to new ways of thinking?	Build capacity for individuals to develop a collective understanding of individual and collective responsibilities as social justice leaders.
Anthropology	What physical, historical, and cultural artifacts represent the actions of humans and societies? What rituals and traditions underlie cultures of leadership?	Dismantle the foundational caste system by incorporating the power of cultural ways of knowing, being, and doing.
Philosophy	Why are we doing this? Is it right? What is our moral code, and how do we enact our beliefs about power and privilege?	Reframe the current context by addressing gender and racial issues as moral imperatives to take socially just actions.
Politics	What power dynamics impact decisions? How can we better manage the micropolitical contexts?	Redirect the micropolitical by realigning power dynamics to support equitable and inclusive policies and fully engage the voices of all constituents, including students.

Because a central goal of schooling is preparing citizens in a democracy, modeling a pluralistic society in educational settings means that all community members should share responsibility for contributing to the public discourse and developing and implementing goals and outcomes. Therefore, *leading and learning* is an accurate description of school leaders' role *and* an expression of a philosophical commitment to the value of democratic education. However, hierarchical—positional and political power—leadership has proved unable to achieve these ends. We depart from this historical and systemic tradition of leadership and offer a leadership pivot that is more inclusive, engaging (circular), and focused on social justice. These leaders focus on social justice as the moral imperative of their work and use social justice principles and practices side by side with colleagues to design and implement change efforts. The evidence we present from our work with school and district leaders helped us document and reimagine their roles as leaders committed to enacting circular and social justice leadership.

CIRCULAR LEADERSHIP

The hallmark of the current educational policy panorama is the faith placed in school and district leaders to improve schools, which policymakers promote as a critical lever for school change (Grissom et al., 2021). Given that "school leadership has a significant effect on features of the school organization which positively influences the quality of teaching and learning" (Leithwood et al., 2020, p. 6), such faith is understandable. Indeed, the crucial roles that school or district leaders play in charting school improvement plans that sustain durable and equitable student outcomes are undisputed (Allensworth & Hart, 2018; Leithwood & Louis, 2012; Grissom et al., 2013).

However, most leaders limit their possibilities by depending on a traditional approach—"top-down control and few degrees of freedom" (Gutiérrez, 2016, p. 190). This leadership tradition leads to egg cartons (Lortie, 1975), fiefdoms (Tyack & Cuban, 1997), norms of privacy (Little, 1990), microsystems (Rowan, 1990), silos (Militello et al., 2009), and ignoring the cultural ways of learning that we know support all learners (Gay, 2000; Hammond, 2015; Peltier, 2021). An alternative perspective for leadership, based on lessons from Native/Indigenous ways of knowing, is not just necessary but can galvanize a way forward (Benham & Cooper, 2000; Mitchell, 2018). Through lessons and story, leadership can be conceived differently: "Hollywood had it wrong when the White man said, 'Take me to your leader,' and he was promptly taken to Chief Eagle Eye. Instead, he might have been taken to the tribal council" (Benham & Napier, 2002, p. 142). Similarly, we seek to shift from the leader as a single, heroic individual who reinforces—often unwittingly—the status quo (Kim & Mauldin, 2022) to more expansive and inclusive leadership. In the language of Mi'kmaq scholars Battiste and Henderson (2020), the "dreamers, workers, and professionals should [collaboratively] build creative, effective institutions and programs for their people" (p. iii) to cultivate a renaissance for schools and institutions (ᐃᐣᑯᐃgᐁᓈᐢ ᕒᐁᓇᐃᐢᓴᐣᒉ). Thus, we need a pivot from leader as a person to leadership as a function—a circular function in which many can participate.

Reliance on individual leaders who are often inadequately supported drains leaders' personal and professional resources and is unsustainable (Bottery, 2016; Honig, 2012; Wang, 2021). Although principals' actions help to drive teacher improvement and student achievement, schools do not improve solely based on strong principals (Sebastian et al., 2014). Without necessary reciprocity among all organizational actors, no amount of effort by one person purportedly "in charge" can achieve more equitable student learning results. Some term this response horizontal leadership; we prefer to name it circular leadership—nonhierarchical leadership that values the voices of everyone in the veritable circle of adults who bear responsibility for leading and learning and who work together to learn together, solve conflicts, and achieve goals.

There are 90,000+ public school principals in the United States; with assistant principals and district supervisors, they represent a critical resource for change in schools. However, their success depends on reimagining how to address the academic, social-emotional, and civic goals of schooling more equitably. Individuals in formal administrative roles in education need to mesh their current knowledge, skills, and dispositions with alternative ways of thinking and facilitating so that school and district leadership looks differently—a mashup that requires they look to untapped resources to rethink and remake leadership practices. Thus, the designated leader must nurture a frame of mind and garner the capacity to engage others in the complex task of reciprocal learning and leading.

In Grubb's (2009) typology of school resources [Resource 1A], abstract resources—trust, collective power, and information—constitute critical conditions for doing the complex work of school change. Those resources, in combination with others, affect student outcomes. Of course, increased funding for schools is critical as education budgets continue to shrink, but without attention to complex, compound, and abstract resources in schools, additional money resources make little to no difference in schooling outcomes. The "complex and abstract resources must be constructed by teachers and leaders working collectively at the school level without much money but with other resources (leadership, collaboration, and vision)" (p. 88).

A latent but valuable abstract resource—hidden in plain sight—is leadership as the function of many who collectively lead reform efforts (Bohannon et al., 2024). Spillane et al. (2001) define distributed leadership as a group composed of all leaders necessary to address a particular task: "School leaders' knowledge and expertise may be best explored at the group or collective level rather than at the individual level" (p. 25). Gronn (2002) argues that distributed leadership is additive—since every adult is a leader; the totality of leaders' work adds up to more than the sum of its parts. The distributed lens provides a different viewpoint, not one of leader as a "great man" (Rost, 1991), "hero," (Gronn, 2003), or the delegator of responsibilities. As Schön (1987) stated, "I am presumed to know but I am not the only one in this situation to have relevant and important knowledge" (p. 300). In healthy organizations, everyone leads; sound leadership is encouraged by good ideas, not a reliance on positional power (March, 1997).

In addition, we propose rethinking data use as a resource. Too often, data are weaponized in educational settings; autopsy achievement data are decontextualized and used as noise to obfuscate change. Using data is not simply the pro forma activity of dragging out last year's achievement data or disproportionate discipline data. At a typical August faculty meeting, teachers shrug, pour over the data, discuss the compounding and confounding issues, return to classrooms, and do not change—not because they do not want to, but because there is no process for authentic evidence-based change. The roadmap from the achievement gap graph to changing practices in schools or classrooms remains unclear. As an antidote, our schools are replete with useful data that practitioner-researchers can filter, analyze, disaggregate, and contextualize—and act on differently.

When school constituents have time and processes to think about which school data are helpful, they can use the evidence from the data analysis to leverage iterative change in individual classrooms and schoolwide. Petrides and Guiney (2002) utilize an ecological model of knowledge management to make data more attainable, usable, and meaningful for practitioners: "Knowledge management brings together three core organizational resources—people, processes and technologies" (p. 10). We urge school and district constituents to experiment and improve by converting daily and iterative data to usable evidence to uncover equity issues, have conversations, make decisions, and act.

Untapped leadership resources exist in the very neighborhood of the problem. That is, the "people closest to the issues are best situated to discover answers to local concerns" (Guajardo et al., 2016, p. 25). School and district constituents and their ideas are abstract resources that are traditionally overlooked or marginalized. Our vision of *leading and learning* is circular rather than horizontal or vertical because we believe that leadership for equity requires the wisdom and efforts of multiple actors working collectively in conversation with each other—not a sole wise leader directing the work of others (hierarchical) or individuals in parallel leadership positions making decisions without consulting one another ("flattening the hierarchy"). That said, there is an inherent tension in recommending nonhierarchical leadership in schools and districts that are so obviously and persistently hierarchical. In this system, principals work as middle managers with multiple administrative layers above them; their work is shaped by district, state, and national priorities, and the direction over which a single principal acting alone has little influence (Flessa, 2012). Yet, a single leader can redefine relationships to encourage co-inquiry and co-learning and, as a result, have more influence with teachers, students, and families than acting alone.

Effectively engaging in nonhierarchical leadership work within explicitly hierarchical organizations requires different skills and dispositions. Specifically, circular leadership means applying the lessons from the growing literature base about central office leadership, namely that school-level improvement is more likely when schools have key support of central offices rather than administrative interference (Goldring et al., 2020; Honig & Rainy, 2020; Woulfin & Weiner, 2017). By *leading and learning* differently, leaders engage all voices, especially those of historically marginalized persons, including the voices of community elders and youth (Dei et al., 2022; Khalifa, 2018; Radd et al., 2020). Enacting circular leadership means engaging all constituents as practitioner-researchers to collect and analyze evidence to support inclusive decision-making—thus liberating decisions from the purview of just a few in positions of power. Change means broadening the idea of who is involved and who makes decisions.

LEADERSHIP FOR SOCIAL JUSTICE

For us, effective leadership is not a set of technical skills alone; *leading and learning* means acquiring the knowledge, skills, and dispositions that serve social justice goals. The goals are not sentiments; they are actions that require redistributing educational opportunity to those who have been denied it. Leading and learning should be judged by how collective efforts are channeled toward shared equity goals, which requires attention to culturally responsive practices. In their examination of the scholarship on culturally responsive school leadership (CRSL), Khalifa et al. (2016) concluded that four strands emerge from the relevant literature: (1) developing critical self-awareness; (2) including all members of the community, (3) attending to culturally responsive school environments, and (4) promoting community advocacy. Restoule (2017) found a similarity in Indigenous education in that "learning takes place in the community and the environment, and everyone is a potential teacher" (p. 3). This kind of leadership requires an awareness of the cultural ways of knowing and acting that we learn and actualize and how, through reflection, we can change those ways of acting. Morris (2023) reminds us that we must recognize systems of oppression and our roles—often unwitting—in supporting them. As a result of reflection, we can seize opportunities to interrupt and disrupt. As groups of practitioner-researchers, they can engage in justice-centered practices in which they challenge notions of power and expertise, support culturally sustaining practices, and decenter Whiteness values and practices in education (Wetzel et al., 2023).

Praxis, deep and intentional reflection to act, is vital for enacting our espoused values of equity and justice and engaging others in the doing and learning process (Argyris & Schön, 1974, 1978; Freire, 1970). Surfacing conflicting views encourages participation in designing and implementing collaborative goals (Anderson, 1996). In addition, emotional well-being is critical in troubled times, and a trusting school climate is a binding and mediating influence on achieving equitable student academic goals (Sebastian & Allensworth, 2019). While individual self-care is essential, a network of supportive colleagues who maintain collective care contributes to a strong and resilient school climate (Aguilar, 2018; Theoharis, 2024; Velasco, 2021). Successful leadership—the kind of leadership that happens in supportive circles of care—attends to deep reflection and participants' social-emotional needs. This type of deep reflection based on critical consciousness builds the muscle for social justice leadership and maintaining radical hope (Lear, 2006; Roberts, 2023).

In harnessing collective efforts, school or district constituents must be explicit about their equity goals, identify how micro actions contribute to the macro or structural, and be clear about the next steps to fully enact their values and interrupt inequitable practices (Rigby & Tredway, 2015). The school community members must be ready to be warm demanders of each other regarding equity actions and hold firm to their values of antiracist, inclusive educational practices (Bondy & Ross, 2008; Bondy et al., 2017; Delpit, 2012; Kendi, 2019). They must be ready to re-examine traditional societal roles and actions and adopt more culturally responsive practices.

While we have refined, practiced, and published processes that support circular and social justice leadership, we do not pretend to own pedagogies and practices that precede us. Many engaging, community-based strategies come from diverse cultural practices, ancestral practices, and the lessons of our mothers, grandfathers, friends, fellow scholars, practitioners, students, and other colleagues doing similar work. Our quest here is to present a set of critical principles and practices that we have borrowed, witnessed, and used in our work. While the evidence from schools and districts confirms these elements are useful for taking charge of leading and learning in your context, we encourage adaptations and detail the resources and protocols at the conclusion of each chapter.

CONCLUSION

Our notion of leading and learning diverges from simple solutions and focuses on what actually could happen in the mystery black box of teaching and learning (Cuban, 2013). We open the black box of leadership to understand the dispositions, knowledge, and practices that need to be exposed, refined, and reimagined to ensure socially just learning experiences for students. As we suggested at the start of this chapter, our approach evolves from a mashup of traditional and new knowledge and practices. We look to the values of improvisation as a necessary philosophy and process of learning and then leading differently (March, 1988; Nachmanovitch, 1991), which is captured in the liberatory design thinking of experimentation and probing (Anaissie et al., 2021). By valuing a place of uncertainty, leaders can reinvent solutions to thorny, complex issues in schools and districts (Jackson, 2023). We urge you to imagine a mashup that entails weaving people and places with processes to craft potent possibilities for equitable results in your context.

School and district leaders remain in the spotlight and are responsible for facilitating change. However, relying on the single designated leader as the sole decision-maker must shift from the power of one to the power of many. A compelling mashup requires artistry by melding craft, art, and science to pave the way toward *leading and learning*. Only then can authentic collective leadership manifest itself to iteratively inform practices in schools and districts. We surface and make a case for leadership as a function in a school and district that is shared by many and operates in ways that draw on the benefits of collective teaching, learning, and leading. Such leadership—based on collective resources, asset-informed tools, and evidence—offers an abundance of possibilities for activating the goal of this dissertation title: *To leave this place better than you found it* (James, 2023). To do so, circular and social justice leadership offers a theory and practices for garnering the important resource for change—the critical insights and vantage points that constituents in schools and districts can bring communities to lead and learn together.

RESOURCES AND TOOLS FOR CHAPTER 1

https://www.tcpress.com/filebin/PDFs/9780807786147_supp.pdf
(See page 7 for a QR code linking to this URL.)
1A. Typology of Resources

CHAPTER 2

The Pedagogy of Trust

Setting the Necessary Conditions

> Relationships are built at the speed of trust, and social change happens at the speed of relationships.
>
> Jennifer Bailey (2019)

Cultivating relational trust *from within* is a primary resource for leading and learning. Change comes from *within* each person; however, cultivating trust among members of any group creates a communal spirit *within* an organizational entity—a classroom, a school, or a district—that speeds up social change in schools and communities. A pedagogy of trust provides a powerful undercurrent of intentional practices that promote relational trust as an ongoing process, not a destination—embedding ways of being in a community that underline the value of democratic participation. Like cultivating a garden, organizational actors must be vigilant about weeding out potential impediments and buffering and brokering outside forces that can fragment or neutralize school improvement from within. Creating and sustaining relational trust is an ongoing, incremental process. If leaders are strongly committed to shared values and coherent practices, they have processes for activating and actualizing trust as a necessary condition for school reform. We offer a set of practices to build, deepen, and strengthen the bonds of the organizational actors whose common goal is fostering just outcomes for student academic, social-emotional, and civic learning.

Trust, built and sustained over time, is a resource for change. Butler and Cantrell (1984) name five dimensions of trust:

> (1) integrity, honesty, and truthfulness; (2) competence, technical and interpersonal knowledge, and skills required to do one's job; (3) consistency, reliability, predictability, and good judgment in handling situations; (4) loyalty or benevolent motives [and actions] and willingness to save face of other person; (5) openness or mental accessibility, willingness to share ideas and information freely. (p. 19)

As discussed in Chapter 1, Grubb (2009) cites relational trust as an abstract resource in schools that mitigates dynamic inequality, a continuing issue in school reform efforts that explains how inequitable practices foster exponential inequality. Trust cannot be "bought"; as an abstract resource, it is intangible—it cannot be held or seen, but it is discernable among organizational actors. In the multiple individual and group interactions that form the complex web of school or district relationships (teacher to teacher; principal/AP to teacher, teacher to parent; teacher to students, district supervisor to principal, etc.), trust needs to permeate interactions. Tschannen-Moran (2014) and Tschannen-Moran and Hoy (2000) describe trust as an ethic of mutual care and equity bolstered by respect, authenticity, openness, and honesty that a group establishes through mutual obligations and expectations and a willingness to be vulnerable and take risks. Bryk and Schneider (2002) identified relational trust as a resource for cultivating and sustaining a community and a crucial factor in repairing trust when conflict occurs; Bryk et al. (2010) determined the absolute necessity of relational trust to any school improvement process [Resource 2A for relational trust].

Based on over 20 years of work with school leaders and their teams, we have developed and refined a set of practices that fortify and sustain a pedagogy of trust in school communities—and, for that matter, all types of communities—to engage with each other and make collaborative decisions. As school leaders establish and sustain the conditions for trust by paying careful attention to pedagogical approaches to build and sustain trust, they surface and have conversations to resolve productive conflict. By being intentional, we establish and maintain the necessary conditions for effective leading and learning as a school community—a critical component of achieving the desired equitable outcomes of just schools. When groups have a high degree of relational trust, they can accelerate school change efforts.

As instructors of educators and facilitators of change efforts in schools, we hear positive responses from activities that solicit deep trust and learning. Such activities are necessary to develop a critical consciousness (Radd et al., 2021), a necessary ingredient for leading with a culturally responsive stance (Hammond, 2015; Khalifa, 2018; Ladson-Billings, 2014). As we describe the pedagogy of trust through protocols for deep learning about self and others, we highlight gracious space, dynamic mindfulness, and arts integration as foundational scaffolding elements that promote the necessary conditions for change. We offer personal narrative protocols that support and sustain relational trust as a critical element of working together in schools, districts, and communities. Finally, we discuss how to organize more productive meetings that always include protocols that nurture trust.

GRACIOUS SPACE

Gracious space is defined as "a spirit and setting where we invite the 'stranger' and embrace 'learning in public'" (Hughes & Grace, 2011, p. 11). Establishing a holding space—a gathering—in which adults can feel cared for and care for others is an essential factor for supporting relational trust; in such a space, adult learners can identify and develop the gifts they bring to the work as we learn and lead collectively (Drago-Severson, 2012; Drago-Severson et al., 2023). Others name gracious space as a brave or necessary space (Brown, 2018; Quadros-Meis, 2021) or an *espacio sano* (Velasco, 2021), a healthy space for leaders and teachers to practice self-care so that they can continue becoming the social justice leaders they purport to value. As leaders understand and practice the four elements of gracious space—spirit, setting, inviting the stranger, and learning in public—they develop a holding space for change efforts.

Bringing the **spirit** of gracious space to any place means welcoming each other to participate fully, both as individuals and as a collective. Prija Parker (2018) urges us to understand our purpose in gathering and to recognize that how we gather matters. The spirit of gracious space is grounded in intentionality, compassion, and curiosity. When we bring these elements into relationships and collective spaces, we are "being" and enacting gracious space. Gracious space has a physical dimension, **setting**, that can support or impede our ability to feel productive, healthy, and connected with our work and with others. Gracious space appeals to the five senses and encourages a spirit of the sixth sense of intuition, creativity, and imagination. Paying attention to simple hospitality (local food and drink) and items that reflect the cultural context creates a welcoming and inclusive space that encourages interaction. Attending to physical and emotional needs so that participants have equitable access to participation is critical.

Gracious space shifts to a "systems" perspective when we **invite the "stranger."** Borrowed from Parker Palmer (1983), the term "stranger" refers to any individual we do not typically know or interact with—someone with a different background, perspective, race, gender, culture, ability, sexual orientation, geographic origin, or any other quality that may make the person seem different. Inviting the stranger also means being open to a new idea or perspective. We need the stranger inside us and ideas from others when considering complexity and innovation, which provide multiple perspectives before deciding on a course of action. Embracing the stranger helps us "move beyond tolerance of differences" (Hughes & Grace, 2011, p. 30) to enact real change, which is developmental, takes time, and is diffused when people observe, try, and find relative advantage (Drago-Severson et al., 2023; Rogers, 2003).

To address the system by incorporating gracious space as a practice, we apply deep listening and learning as we **learn in public**, which requires humility, a willingness to explore assumptions, letting go of the "right way" of doing things, and being willing to change one's mind. To fully incorporate gracious space, we learn in public by making mistakes, trying out ideas that are not fully formed, and accepting how learning occurs as participants verbalize their ideas [Resources 2B and 2C].

In a gracious space, we change interactive dynamics. We listen, not to respond, judge, or gain an advantage, but to learn—we witness with curiosity (Machado, 2021; see Figure 2.1). This requires generosity of spirit and humility—a willingness to explore assumptions, let go of the "right way," change one's mind, and be aware that participants often try out ideas as they formulate their initial thinking. That sometimes requires admitting mistakes and often apologizing. We choose graciousness by being open-minded and welcoming diverse opinions. This requires the courage of vulnerability and provides a pathway to harness conflict to design creative solutions.

Figure 2.1. Continuum of Effective Listening

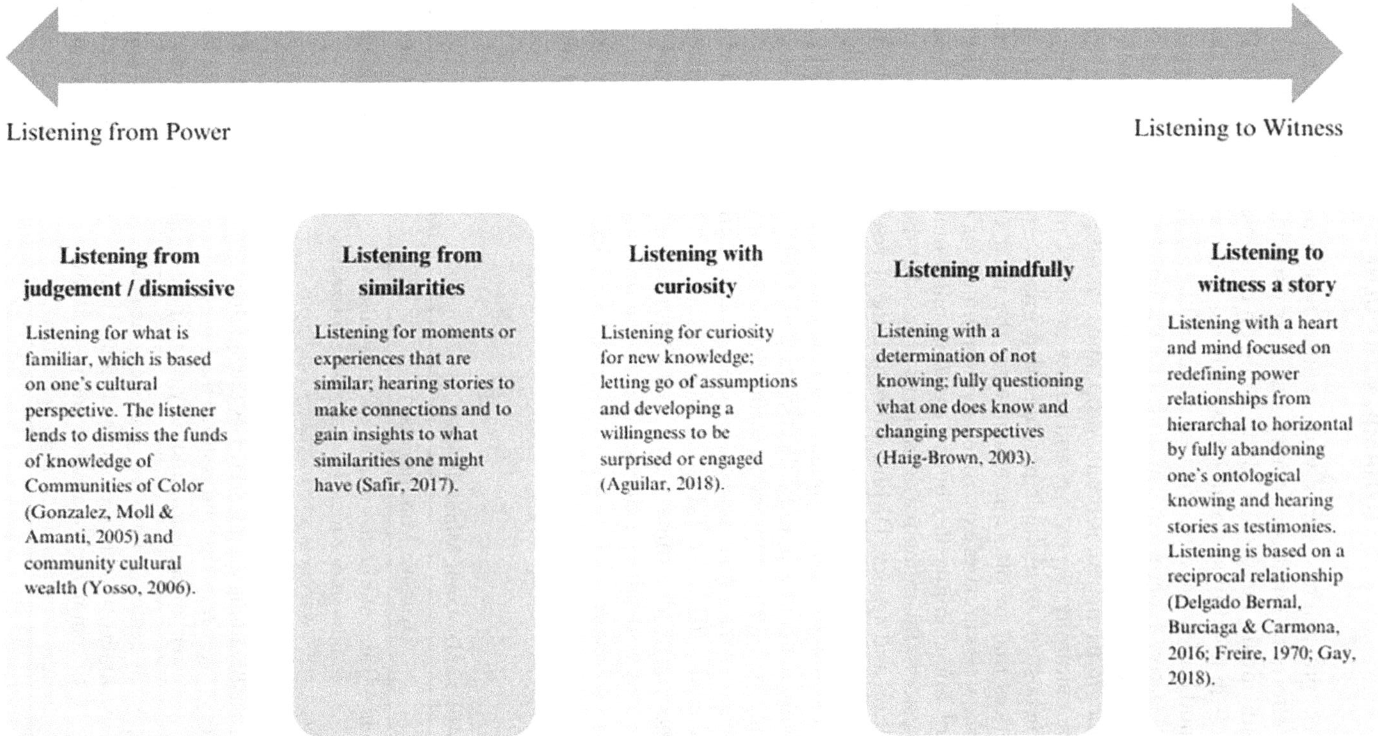

Courtesy of Moraima Machado.

DYNAMIC MINDFULNESS

Mindfulness practice has gained wide popularity as a powerful tool for supporting collective efforts to build community and offer participants ways to recognize and nurture individuals and groups. By focusing on dynamic mindfulness (DMind)—or movement—in mindfulness practice, we address root causes of issues that students, teachers, and leaders have experienced and continue to experience in oppressive social systems. Negative experiences can settle into the body epigenetically or physically—"our issues are in our tissues" (Bose et al., 2017). Critical flash points underscore why DMind, in particular, is broad, deep, and effective; it is evidence based, trauma responsive, culturally responsive, and equity-driven (Duane et al., 2021).

In a meta study of multiple practices that improve executive function, mindfulness practices that involve movement were the most effective (Diamond & Ling, 2016). Since stress impairs executive function (functions related to working memory, self-control, and cognitive flexibility), dynamic mindfulness offers the best results for addressing stress. By urging participants to proceed at their chosen pace to build self-determination and agency, DMind offers healing by re-engaging the body and mind to calm anxiety and manage triggers that often result from culturally oppressive practices. DMind addresses equitable and inclusive school outcomes by adding the critical components of self and collective care and supports individuals in persisting and resisting systems of oppression through collective action.

The ABCs of mindful practices include action, breathing, and centering (adapted from Bose et al., 2017; see Table 2.1 and [Resource 2D]). Action means attending to body movement. Breathing decreases the fight-or-flight response and restores the ability to focus and fully participate. Centering increases observing in community and ensures we make mindful and culturally responsive choices. We start meetings with DMind and propose that leaders and teachers use DMind in meetings and classrooms.

Table 2.1. ABCs of Dynamic Mindfulness

	Dynamic Mindfulness	Implications
Actions and Mindful Movements	Using our bodies to address stress and trauma in our muscles and tissues increases self-awareness and increases equitable access for increased student readiness.	**Increase equitable ACCESS to learning.**
Breathing Techniques	Breathing deeply decreases the fight-or-flight response and restores the ability to listen, think, learn, and fully participate.	**Focus on BREATHING joy and justice into schools and communities**
Centering Practices	By centering ourselves, we strengthen our ability to take care of ourselves and listen in community to another and to collectively address systemic barriers to learning.	**CENTER on collective care to learn, teach, and lead for social justice.**

ARTS INTEGRATION

Similar to mindfulness, the arts offer a resource that (1) responds to the neuroscience explosion of knowledge about brain-based learning, (2) supports us in understanding how anxiety that is a result of stereotype threat affects cognition (Steele, 2010), and (3) reinforces culture as a crucial component of information processing (Hammond, 2015). Arts integration as a practice supports building and sustaining trust. As Pink (2006) suggests, the emphasis on right-brain learning comports with the knowledge and skills necessary for 21st-century global citizens because the right brain–left brain "collaboration" offers simultaneity, large context, and big picture thinking to complement sequential and detail emphases. Second, attention of adults or K–12 students is often compromised in learning situations because they feel a stereotype threat related to microaggressions. Using the arts as a pedagogical tool offers facilitators and teachers ways to calm the amygdala so that everyone can fully engage in learning. Finally, information processing for many learners—adults and students—is an equitable access issue if the information or learning is not culturally responsive. Using visual, musical, literary, and performance arts as a mainstay of our work helps us maintain equitable access and set a gracious table for developing relationship trust.

When participants in learning situations (graduate classes, faculty meetings, or K–12 classrooms) visually represent their thinking and learning, they integrate brain functions, which increases coherent learning. To support arts integration in practice, protocols employ artistic choices as stimuli for personal narratives—stories that represent our current and historical self. When we teach graduate classes, each class assignment includes an arts integration activity that connects to the reading content. We routinely use several tools and protocols that fortify relational trust through arts and visual representations [Tools 2H and 2I]. However, because of copyright issues, we invite you to find and use visual images that you may find useful as we cannot include all of our protocols with art on the website.

PERSONAL NARRATIVES

Initially, we build trust through telling stories—or personal narratives—that help us understand our histories, identities, ideas, hopes, and dreams (Tredway et al., 2020). Storytelling—termed testimonio or plática—offers a way to connect and liberate the power of the many. When we tell stories, we amplify trust because everyone has an equal seat at the table—we ground our stories via the personal narratives in our journeys to be and become teachers and leaders of equity in schools and districts. A rationale for storytelling that we find important: Once a person shares a deep story with even one other person, they feel a sense of community—and contribute to the story of us and the story of an equitable community (Ganz, 2011) [Tool 2F].

We start each online or in-person meeting, event, or class with a personal narrative and use literary, visual, or musical art as the catalyst for thinking and storytelling. The personal narrative is definitely not a typical icebreaker activity. Instead, the narratives we chose offer an affective and cognitive hook for the learning goals as well as an opportunity to ground our stories in the goals of equity and social justice. In other words, they offer a specific, intentional anticipatory set that sets the stage for discussion and learning.

For example, we facilitate wisdom circles to learn about community stories. Integrating arts as a personal narrative choice, we use the song "Somebody Prayed Me Over" from Sweet Honey in the Rock, an *a capella* Black women's singing group founded by Bernice Reagan Johnson [Tool 2H]. As participants listen to the lyrics and reflect on who supported their life journeys, they share a story in dyads or trios. Such connections set the stage for engagement, and the text of the stories becomes an impetus for understanding each other and firmly establishing a gracious space for learning. In identifying specific types of personal narratives, we urge you to see examples on the website: https://www.tcpress.com/filebin/PDFs/9780807786147_supp.pdf

Emulation Poems and Endowed Objects

To emulate is to copy or use as a guide. We choose poems with repetitive features that are useful for emulating. Each participant listens to the facilitator's example and writes a poem to share with a partner or trio. For example, we adapted the "I Am From," a form of emulation writing developed originally by Linda Christensen (2009), to include these prompts: *I come from a place where . . . ; I am in a place where . . . ; and I am going to a place where.* We model our emulation poems and invite others to do so [Tool 2F].

The purpose of using an endowed object is similar to the emulation poem—to hear a story about an object that is significant to the individual. The use of an endowed object originates from the theater—characters handle props that have great meaning to them—the king's crown or the magic sword. In choosing an object, each person endows the object with meaning to represent vis-à-vis the object something tangible and meaningful. Some objects are symbolic metaphors for life events, relationships, and qualities people value. Others are ordinary objects that have personal significance to the storytellers. Sharing in a circle and placing the objects in the circle creates a collective sense of bringing a part of self to the group.

Autobiographies

In sharing an autobiography or memoir, persons represent a part of their lives. Some of us have integrated our many selves into a more coherent picture; in other cases, internal conflicts still define how we interpret ourselves. Many have had startling events—even traumas—that play a large role in our life trajectory. Still others have had conflicts of conscience with people near and dear to us or conflicts in the workplace. We use autobiographies to interrogate how we navigate the social complexity in society and our workplaces (Gooden & Dantley, 2012; Singleton, 2015).

Journey Lines

A journey line represents a specific autobiographical story; each participant constructs a "story of self" chronologically (earliest memory to the present). Shared journey lines become the "story of us" or a public narrative, which in turn can inform a "story of collective action" about a particular topic (Ganz, 2011). The choice of topic for a journey line should relate to the purpose of a group or a particular gathering or meeting. Examples include:

- Journey line of COURAGE
- Journey line of CHANGE
- Journey line of TEACHING
- Journey line of TEAMING
- Journey line of LEADERSHIP
- Journey line of READING
- Journey line of EVALUATION

We all have journey lines that prompted us to become teachers and leaders [Tool 2E].

We share other examples of journey lines that demonstrate the transparency and vulnerability vital for establishing and maintaining the trust that undergirds our work and the work of school reform. Tables 2.2, 2.3, and 2.4 are our journey lines.

Mandalas

A mandala is a visual representation—a spiritual guiding tool—useful in understanding what influenced a person in becoming who they are at a moment in time. To create the visual map of the mandala, participants engage in a guided inquiry about their personal and professional selves—understanding how self requires inquiry and reflection and imagining how our various selves intersect (Figure 2.2; [Tool 2G]). Sharing mandalas helps participants think about purpose and how stories (storyline, relationships) inform our community participation and moral imperatives (Herman, 2013).

Digital Stories

Digital storytelling provides an alternative storytelling method. Digital stories "give rise to the aesthetics of voice" (Militello & Guajardo, 2013, p. 83). Lambert (2002) suggests that by telling personal and communal stories, we create an empathetic bond among ourselves. Hoggan and Militello (2015) stated,

> Realizing one's tacit assumptions and narratives is very difficult, and therefore, artistic endeavors are often useful as a means to elicit and convey them. Through the creation of a digital story, students are asked to reflect on and depict a narrative they have about themselves and then to depict that narrative through video. (p. 121)

Table 2.2. Lynda: Journey Line of Courage

1959	Stand up for a friend accused of cheating in 7th grade
1964	American Legion contest speech on civil rights
1967	Figured out how to survive a complex situation
1971	May Day nonviolent civil disobedience against the war
1983	Arrested—South African embassy protest
1988	Breast cancer survivor

Table 2.3. Matt: Journey Line of Leadership

Adolescence	Enrolled in a ballet class with a friend who was anxious about attending as the only male
High School	Attended Michigan Boy's State; named captain of the varsity football and basketball teams
College	Big Brother and coach at local agencies while a student at the University of Michigan
Early Career	Became a school principal at the age of 29
2014	Assumes an endowed chair position at East Carolina University

Table 2.4. Joe: Journey Line of Teaching, Learning, and Leading

Childhood in Ohio	School as a place for curiosity, independence, and growth; conformity and fear Gay kid in a conservative time and place—quickly learning and following unwritten rules
Teaching in Texas	New teacher with limited preparation: learning how to ask for help, be strict but not mean, well prepared but responsive, authentic, and connect with families' assets and strengths
Teaching and Leading in Mexico	Personal niceness is not sufficient for effective school administration Learn a second language Life-changing
Graduate School in California	Integrating rigorous intellectual inquiry and practical application Reciprocal responsibility and accountability required as a peer sex educator volunteer work at the Gay Men's Health Collective
Immigrating to Canada	As a newcomer to Canada, particular responsibilities to truth and reconciliation School leadership research and practice is a fruitful, engaging, rigorous field beyond U.S. hegemony

Figure 2.2. Mandala Elements

Courtesy of Maenette K. P. Benham.

Because many learners today are digital natives, telling stories in a digital format is accessible. Other participants may need new skills, but the product quality is less critical than the stories. We use digital stories for individual autobiographies and telling the stories of a community or a specific project. For individuals, the digital story typically includes the "geography of self," the historical, biological, cultural, and political self (see Figure 2.3). Sharing digital stories in small groups prompts discussion and intersections about identity, histories, and values.

Personal connections as a routine part of our work are critical to cultivating and sustaining relational trust so that we have experiences that "arouse curiosity, strengthen initiative and set up desires and purposes to carry a person over dead places in the future" (Dewey, 1938, p. 38). Often, those dead places emerge as areas of conflict, and bonds of relational trust help us navigate differences of opinion and figure out how to cooperate.

ADDRESSING CONFLICT

Organizational citizens have obligations to enact values of cooperation and collaboration (Tschannen-Moran & Hoy, 2000); however, at times, those commitments break down, and micro-level power dynamics threaten the climate of mutuality. Because constituents in schools are "constantly engaged in the process of discerning the intentions embedded in the actions of others" (Bryk & Schneider, 2002, p. 138), mistrust is sometimes an outcome. Before a conflict arises, groups should consider processes for addressing internal conflicts or external threats to the organization. In addition, when groups encounter dilemmas or problems in implementing change, processes help them respond to the dilemma or settle disputes.

Being intentional about meeting agreements and how a group might solve issues or conflicts before issues arise is a reasonable idea for sustaining relational

Figure 2.3. Geography of Self

Historical SELF	**Biological SELF**
What major historical events (micro or macro) impacted your life? What local (micro) and larger (macro) events have been close to you spatially, geographically, physically, and emotionally? What is significant about the geographic spaces (power of place) that you live in currently or lived in historically? If you have access to information, do a generational analysis (your ancestors) of what brought you to the place/space in which you find yourself. What were your first experiences in understanding race and diversity?	Describe your physical makeup and genetic composition and, from what you currently know, elaborate on where you come from (e.g., father, mother, grandparents, etc.). Present pictures of yourself as a youth and compare them to the present; how have you changed? What is your genetic make-up and how do you identify yourself? What do you see as your dominant composition and prominent characteristics? If you have children or know your relatives, do you see this in other relatives or your children?
Cultural SELF	**Political SELF**
How has your ethnic, social, and cultural self defined who you are? How has/does your racial or physical identity interact or connect to the communities where you live, work, and play? What cultural experiences shaped your values and beliefs? Have cultural experiences as an adult changed your beliefs and values over time? What are the context and conditions that have molded your cultural identity? What does diversity mean to you?	How have local (micro) and national (macro) politics shaped your values and beliefs? How do you deal with conflict? What was your first political action (test your memory)? How do you define power and how do you use it? What does "standing up for justice" mean to you?

trust. Particularly for leaders who experience power asymmetry between the principal and other school groups or roles, leaders need to reduce the sense of vulnerability that others feel (Bryk & Schneider, 2002; Suarez, 2018) to ensure circular leadership. Two processes have been useful: the kiva, an ancient Pueblo circle activity used to solve internal community problems, and the critical friends group (CFG) consultancy, developed by the Annenberg group in the 1980s and improved by the San Francisco Coalition of Essential Small Schools (SF-CESS) [Tool 2J].

A kiva is a circular structure of the Pueblo Indians used for ritual, discussion, or problem solving. In Pueblo culture, the kiva is a gathering used for problem-solving purposes (Middlebrooks, 2008; Pavlik, 2003). Like Suina (2016), we view the kiva as a spiritual space that exemplifies how a democratic space can be a support for reflection and retreat "by opening up and talking to others when you are going through hard times or experiencing stress, but also being there to listen and support others when they are struggling" (p. 76). Based on empowering the voices of many, the process models representative democracy in which participants have multiple opportunities to share responses and question each other. Small groups pose questions and discuss. Then, representatives from small groups come to the center to offer ideas. At the same time, other participants take notes and have a chance to respond in successive small-group discussions.

Another useful form of problem solving is the CFG process. Focusing on "critical" in the sense of vital or important, CFGs offer a structured forum for addressing issues or challenges. As a result, leaders and teachers can have difficult conversations and ground their discussion in larger issues of equity. Peer groups use a structured process to bring an issue to a group and discuss possible ways to address the issue. A regular use of the equity-centered CFG protocol includes a set of equity-focused probing questions, and the presenter of the issue has an opportunity to listen to others and then decide what ideas might be useful (Tool 2J).

ORGANIZATIONAL MEETINGS: IN-PERSON AND VIRTUAL LEARNING EXCHANGES

Every gathering is a political act (Parker, 2018); therefore, intentional planning for the outcomes is necessary for successful learning. Internal power dynamics can affect outcomes, and managing those dynamics through grounding in practices supports democratic decision-making (Mitchell, 2018). We often hear that we need more time to get to the main part or outcome of any meeting. Our response: What you do not need is what happens when you do not attend to the practices that hold space for people, their emotions, their ideas, and their stories. Thus, designing effective agendas that intentionally forward the practices we discussed in this chapter can deepen and strengthen relational bonds and simultaneously connect to the meeting goals. A personal narrative is possible in a few minutes using the appreciative listening protocol (Tool 2K)—paired conversations of 2 minutes per person while the other person listens carefully even if the person talking is quiet. Because attendees have made personal connections and are committed to reflection, they "show up" in the space as organizational citizens ready to have a dialogue.

Planning effective meetings means (1) attention to clear outcomes, agreements, and roles for facilitation and participation; (2) a perceptible throughline; (3) appropriate protocols; and (4) time for critical reflection. Too often, meetings are comprised of information we could share via email or in another format or the dreaded slide deck while someone reads information to us. When we prepare for meetings or conference sessions, we ask ourselves what Freire (1970) would think and do. How do we avoid banking method meeting processes and ensure dialogical learning? How might Dewey (1938) assess our ability to model experiential learning? Dynamic mindfulness and personal narratives are necessary components of every meeting because they further the pedagogy of trust, but concerted attention to the dialogue among participants during the meeting is essential for co-constructing meaning and equitably engaging all voices and diverse ideas. For example, one graduate, now a district supervisor, revamped district meetings;

> Each meeting at the district office now includes a personal narrative planned based on the meeting's learning objective. This makes the meeting more personal and supports participant vulnerability. My meetings now have what I call a *Collaborative Meeting Structure* that includes the "what" (content) and the "how" (delivery) for each agenda item. I use CLE protocols regularly to increase engagement, build/sustain relational trust, encourage collaboration, and shift power dynamics. The meetings conclude with a personal reflection. This piece helps encourage metacognition and guides future sessions. (Parker, 2023)

We employed these strategies even during COVID-19, which hit us all hard. Our pivot from online meetings to WebExchanges—mostly eschewing the PowerPoint format—provided facilitators and participants with much-needed time and space for engagement, consultation, and reflection (Tredway et al., 2020). Social-emotional support and interactive learning forums are necessary for the well-being of educators who take care of others and their school community before they take care of themselves. As educators scrambled to establish logistical plans and online learning, we engaged students in ways that did not replicate the didactic nature of online instruction. We used the CLE principles and processes in WebExchanges to incorporate gracious space, dynamic mindfulness, and arts integration. As a result, we developed high-quality learning agendas. Strengthened by digital tools—breakout rooms and online graphic tools—we focused on four elements: relationships and self-care, community building, inquiry, and equitable discourse.

CONCLUSION

We re-emphasize four factors critical to building and sustaining a pedagogy of trust as a necessary condition for all school and district reform work. We urge readers to consider the outcomes for any meeting or project and the throughline necessary to achieve objectives using these elements to plan agendas:

1. **Establish focus:** Begin each session with a welcome and dynamic mindfulness; action, breathing, and centering serve as mechanisms for transition and self-care.
2. **Cultivate relationships:** Through storytelling practices, provide space for personal narratives. Use artistic representations and arts integration to fully engage learners.
3. **Emphasize inquiry:** All learning begins with a focus on self-discovery to reinforce assets and gifts. Endowed objects, autobiographies, and digital stories set up emotional hooks for new learning. Use conversational

protocols in small-group breakouts, virtual or actual learning walks, and private chats. Emphasize experiences using an inquiry model of teaching and learning that re-emphasizes circular leadership.

4. **Engage in equitable discourse:** Utilize specific practices in adult learning that we want in classrooms. Use intentional dialogue structures—think-pair-share, chat boxes or reflection tools, and breakout groups—to ensure that all participants experience equitable access for learning for themselves and others.

Building and sustaining relational trust over time as a necessary condition for improvement requires facilitators—teachers with students or adults with adults—who are facile users of the pedagogy of trust using tools as mediators of cultivating and sustaining relationships. Participants need to feel an emotional and personal commitment to the place and the people before fully committing to *leading and learning together*.

RESOURCES AND TOOLS FOR CHAPTER 2

https://www.tcpress.com/filebin/PDFs/9780807786147_supp.pdf
(See page 7 for a QR code linking to this URL.)

2A. Relational Trust Codes
2B. Gracious Space: Introduction 1
2C. Gracious Space: Introduction 2
2D. Dynamic Mindfulness
2E. Personal Narrative: Journey Lines
2F. Personal Narrative: Emulation Poem
2G. Mandala Process
2H. Arts Integration: Sweet Honey in the Rock
2I. Arts Integration: Ricardo Levins Morales
2J. Critical Friends Consultancy
2K. Appreciative Listening Protocol

CHAPTER 3

Community as Text

Harnessing the Assets of People and Place

> Use the community as a resource to engage students in learning and service and help them become problem solvers and asset builders in their communities.
>
> (Blank et al., 2003, p. 108)

Successful schools invest in authentic and active community engagement. Using the community as a text provides an anchor for fully understanding the history of a place, honoring diverse cultures, and facilitating change efforts that are inclusive of the history and culture. To focus on leadership, learning, and inquiry through the lens of community as text, we define community as a place—a school, a district, an organization, an actual geographic community—committed to social justice outcomes for the members of a designated community. Without diminishing the significant needs in any community, we want leaders and teachers with students and families to recognize the considerable assets that abound in communities. We advocate for harnessing the community as a resource for change by using Community Learning Exchange (CLE) axioms, philosophy, and processes. We underscore that other sources of knowledge in communities should be part of the text for teaching, leading, and learning.

In Lynda's first year of teaching in 1969—one year after the uprisings that followed Dr. King's assassination—she and a teaching partner focused on understanding their middle school students' community. They helped to organize a community newsletter at a public housing development near the school; they made 80 home visits to meet the parents; and they wrote and taught a geography unit of study about the ecological assets and issues in the community. Lynda transferred the processes to a teacher education program and a leadership preparation program at UC Berkeley's Principal Leadership Institute. In collaboration with the Center for Cities in Schools and based on the Y-Plan (McKoy et al., 2022), she and colleagues co-designed a community mapping guide.

As colleagues in facilitating Community Learning Exchanges (CLEs), Matt and Lynda, with others, organized activities based on their commitment to CLE axioms and processes. CLEs are both a set of principles and a process that are adaptable to time and location. Deeply understanding the lived experiences of students and families supports leaders and teachers in connecting those experiences to classroom learning. Culturally responsive instruction relies on knowing students deeply, and teachers and leaders need to engage in mapping so they can use the text of the community as curricular input for instruction. In CLEs, we value culturally responsive and culturally sustaining ways of knowing, storytelling, and an asset-based approach to building and sustaining community. Relationships—individual and group connections—are the foundation of effective school and community change efforts and the learning that must occur to support them. In multiple ways, we emphasize how the people in the community as a geographic place have stories and ideas that provide a text for change efforts.

To discuss the CLE axioms and ecologies of deeply knowing communities (Guajardo et al., 2016), we integrate the philosophy and methods of the Community Learning Exchange with gracious space tenets (see Chapter 2). These foundational elements are the ballast for becoming practitioner-researchers, which we discuss in Chapter 4. As we create spaces where people tell their stories; express their assets, gifts, ideas, and hopes; and together bring about socially just outcomes for our students, CLE axioms and gracious space are touchstones. By assessing the power dynamics in their communities in collective ways, we coalesce the power of many voices as a resource for change (Suarez, 2018). First, we define and describe the CLE axioms that undergird our work and relationships. Then, we explain how Community Learning Exchanges became part of our work and how we developed the capacity and courage to engage the community as text. Finally, we offer some tools for planning and implementing CLEs.

COMMUNITY LEARNING EXCHANGE AXIOMS

The main principles or axioms of a Community Learning Exchange spotlight the power of place and the wisdom of people. The place or community could be a school, an organization, or a particular area of a city, rural area, or community. A place's context (history, politics, culture) is integral to learning about current and historical occupants. By listening to the stories and ideas of community members, we can better reimagine how to engage in school change efforts. Five CLE axioms (Guajardo et al., 2016) anchor our work (see Table 3.1).

In living the CLE axioms, for example, Koh (2023) met with 18 Asian American leaders for 15 months and identified 11 critical tenets of leading with and from their cultural assets. He credits the CLE axioms, ecologies of knowing, and gracious space practices as the key variables supporting leaders to reset the conditions for Asian American leaders as they shifted their views and enacted social change in their contexts. They used counternarratives—their stories and those of historical figures—as a text for developing a community of inquirers to examine themselves and shift leadership in their organizations. Thus, each CLE axiom holds the power because all participants are learners and leaders. Taken together, the axioms provide a philosophy and a tool for holistic engagement with the communities that leaders serve. The axioms are a foundation for coming to know and act at the micro, meso, and macro levels of each community and knowing how to cultivate a gracious space for critical conversations and actions.

Table 3.1. Community Learning Exchange Axioms

Learning and leadership are dynamic social processes.	Learning how to lead and learn within the context of relationships is at the core of leadership and provides the necessary conditions that nurture this development in an inviting and dignified manner. Relationships are the first point of contact, and storytelling and conversations are the mediating tools.
Conversations are critical and central pedagogical processes.	At the core of social learning theory, we create safe spaces and healthy relationships for participants, learners, leaders, and teachers to have conversations and tell stories. If the climate, spirit, and interaction among participants, facilitator, and/or their environment are not inviting and safe, sustainable and public learning is difficult to enact.
The people closest to the issues are best situated to discover answers to local concerns.	Organizing a learning exchange to inform a critical topic or issue is central to the belief that we depend on the voices of many. People find their power and voice in community when they collectively respond to owning their destiny and fostering active agency.
Crossing boundaries enriches the development and educational process.	The ability and willingness to experience a world outside one's daily comfort zone is necessary to break the isolation of people, teams, and organizations. We support boundary crossing that is not limited to geographic borders, economic borders, age, culture and racial borders, gender, faith, and differing abilities.
Hope and change are built on assets and dreams of locals and their communities.	When CLE participants tell their stories, they map their gifts, ideas, hopes, and wishes—garner their ideological, relational, and geographical skills, riches, wishes, and assets for change. As they identify and coalesce their assets, CLE participants view their work and community differently. Issues that have historically been assumptions immediately become opportunities, invitations, and points of action. Transforming one's mind and consciousness from distress and hopelessness to hope and possibilities is, by definition, the most radical transformation we witness during the CLE experience.

ECOLOGIES OF KNOWING

The axioms, which provide a starting point and anchor for change efforts, are nested in three central ecologies of knowing: self, organizations, and communities. The three ecologies represent the focal point of change efforts and organize our thinking and lived experiences from micro to meso to macro levels, or spheres, in which we magnify the lifeworld to humanize the systemsworld (Habermas, 1984; Sergiovanni, 2000). The ecologies have permeable boundaries that leave room for exchange and interplay but serve a critical purpose when making meaning with

Figure 3.1. Ecologies of Knowing and Acting: Self, Organization, and Community

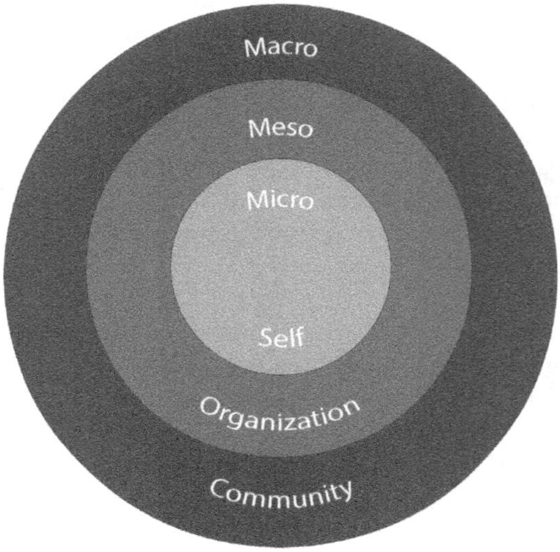

others. What binds the ecologies in any given context is culture—the local mores and traditions of the people in a particular context (Figure 3.1):

- *Self* is the basis of the world of knowing. We must understand ourselves—our multiple identities, particularly within our families—before we can positively contribute to systems.
- *Organization* includes the first tier of systems to which we belong and are responsible—schools and workplaces where we interact with others. We must understand how our collective selves—our lifeworld—can influence organizational practices.
- *Community* encompasses the larger economic, political, spiritual, and cultural world. Understanding the flow of forces and power in our lives and communities is important to inform our work and actions.

The CLE axioms are present at all levels of the ecologies of knowing as we engage leaders with "practice-centered learning experiences that motivate the application of learning" (Cosner et al., 2018, p. 239). CLEs are often events in which we gather. More importantly, CLEs are a way of life—a state of mind to approach work in schools and districts. Using CLE axioms and methods, groups critique the status quo, speak truth to power, celebrate hope, and collaborate to decide on approaches to local problems. The CLE philosophy and practices give participants a new language, a different way of looking at the world, and a network of support that expands their community of practice. In short, reframing our daily conditions from deficits to assets helps build hope and possibilities for change.

Because the CLE is much more than a project or event, the CLE approach challenges our thoughts, actions, practices, and relationships so that they might better support the development of healthier selves, organizations, and communities. We propose learning from lived experiences and authentic and honest relationships of the persons in an organization and/or community. Through Relationships, Assets, Stories, Place, Politics, and Action (RASPPA), CLEs promote practices in which individuals, families, organizations, and communities dream aloud about how to enact leadership and learning (Guajardo & Guajardo, 2013; Guajardo et al., 2016). The CLE approach speaks to a shared radical hope about engaging with others to interrupt oppressive practices:

> Peacemaking . . . is the act of interrupting injustice without mirroring injustice, the act of disarming evil without destroying the evildoer, the act of finding a third way that is neither fight not flight but the careful, arduous pursuit of reconciliation and justice. It is about a revolution of love that is big enough to set both the oppressed and the oppressors free. (Claiborne et al., 2010, p. 58)

We all have work to do to heal the heart of the democracy. By reclaiming matters of the heart, spirit, and local knowledge, the CLE axioms and processes provide a way forward for self and others—if we learn to use our community as the text for leading and learning.

OUR COMMUNITIES AS TEXT

To actualize the axioms in our work, we discuss how Community Learning Exchanges are a philosophy and a process. Text in the context of CLEs can mean the power of cultivating family stories for use in the 5th-grade curriculum (Machado, 2021), mapping a school or community to identify collective assets and identify areas of concern (McKoy et al., 2022), or using counternarratives in an affinity group as Asian American leaders learned to incorporate cultural values in their leadership (Caruz, 2023; Koh, 2023). First, we tell the story of how we "found" one another and how community stories offer a text that has consistently influenced our professional work. Then we discuss the theory and practices of community as text through Community Learning Exchange processes, relying on gracious space as a guide to facilitate dialogue. In the next chapter, we offer specific community mapping tools and examples for engaging in developing community as text.

The work of CLEs, of course, is best accomplished in collaboration with those who hold like values of social justice leadership and a focus on community assets as the starting point of change efforts. Our journey began as Matt, a former principal, worked closely with Maenette Benham in a PhD program and in a grant-funded project, the Kellogg Leadership for Community Change (KLCC). The initial phase of the work focused on six communities seeking to enhance the connections of schools and communities. One of the original KLCC sites was the Llano Grande Center for Research and Development. Llano Grande focused on community engagement in the Rio Grande Valley of southern Texas. There was an instant connection with Miguel and Francisco Guajardo, both academics (University of Texas–Pan American, now Rio Grande Valley and Texas State University) and Maenette (Michigan State University) and Matt (University of Massachusetts after MSU), who asked Chris Janson, counselor educator at the University of North Florida, to join the project. Other colleagues included Kwesi Rollins at Institute for Educational Leadership and Dale Niebow at the Center for Ethical Leadership and home of gracious space.

Over 10 years, the group organized and facilitated 23 Community Learning Exchanges nationwide. As the group convened in 2011 at the Myles Horton Highlander Folk School (later the Highlander Center for Research and Development), the seeds of KLCC solidified the Community Learning Exchange process. Lynda met the group at this event. In 2016, the Guajardo brothers, with Chris and Matt, published the theory and practice of CLEs in *Reframing Community Partnerships in Education: Uniting the Power of Place and Wisdom of People* (Guajardo et al., 2016).

This process exemplifies the importance of relying on others as we fortify our actions with collective learning. We worked with people in different contexts—colleagues, school and district leaders, students—to enact CLEs in similar but not identical ways—all of which linked to systematic academic inquiry with applied action in schools and systems. No one person had all the ideas. That collaboration across time, space, and institutions was fundamental. This kind of work takes time and resources and, importantly, allows for false starts and rethinking. Most of all, this process is an exercise in cultivating and sustaining trust. Our intellectual and activist counterparts work in local places and come together to share and learn together. In essence, our implementation stories provide the text and the anchor for continuing to refine our processes.

The CLE axioms and practices are useful in three ways: (1) philosophical foundation, (2) pedagogical choices, and (3) data construction (hunter et al., 2003)—an iterative process of analyzing data to make decisions. The CLE axioms offer a theoretical framework and a practical guide to creating opportunities for transformative practices to improve schools and communities. In addition, Community Learning Exchanges offer a framework and a methodology for engaging the community in identifying local solutions to local problems or dilemmas. When educational leaders see the community as a critical text for learning, they harness the power of place—recognizing the spaces we occupy, the history and politics, and the wisdom of people—and co-create inclusive spaces by inviting and liberating all voices. Leaders can "empower local people in their own spaces to find solutions that are organic in order to meet the needs of the people that will live in and sustain healthy communities" (Guajardo et al., 2016, p. 9).

By sharing stories that matter, we can change the dominant and sometimes invisible but controlling narrative. Stories—pláticas (Guajardo & Guajardo, 2013) and testimonios (Yosso, 2005)—help us make sense of the world; build and sustain relationships; inform us about context and people other than our own; provide spaces for vulnerability; and give us credibility, courage, and agency when obstacles arise. Stories as counternarratives provide us with possibility and hope. When we share stories, we build collective wisdom and power—once someone hears another person's story, they never see them the same way again. Individual and collective narratives matter as they are the impetus for collective agency and action.

THE ROLE OF STORYTELLING: PLÁTICAS AND TESTIMONIOS

What "texts" do educational leaders need to lead and learn? As school leaders navigate district policies while being bombarded with parental interests, they realize that policies drive compliance while parental influences often drive decision-making (Lareau, 1989). The expansion of social media technologies amplifies public reactions to leadership decisions. How can today's leaders lead school change efforts with these internal and external pressures? With an inquiry mindset and in collaboration, they can harness the stories as assets and data for school change (Guajardo & Guajardo, 2013).

Inquiry, like leadership and learning, can "focus on how local actors orchestrate education interactions for learning [and use] the ideas and tools that *radiate from* the local context of action" (Halverson & Halverson, 2019, p. 7, italics in original). We agree. As leaders learn the processes and tools of practitioner-researchers, they become aware that a community of teachers, staff, and students in their school can provide evidence and ideas for change efforts. And, since schools are nested in institutional, community, economic, and historical contexts, utilizing the power of community as text is an essential support to influence public opinion. As leaders build craft knowledge in which the leader "honors theory, research-based evidence and the wisdom of practice" (Halverson & Halverson, 2019, p. 19), the leader engages others in dialogue so the people closest to the local concern engage in "finding answers and applying those answers to a point of concern" (hunter et al., 2013, p. 17).

To do so, leaders need authentic ways to listen, collaborate, make decisions, implement, evaluate, reflect, and start again. In pre-and in-service preparation, learning traditions are often mandated, abstract, hierarchical, and patriarchal. Furthermore, we have trained leaders to be solution-driven instead of prepared them to be adaptive, equity-centered leaders. Repeatedly, we ask leaders to engage in a process "stimulated by a failure to achieve a goal and continues until it reveals an alternative that is good enough to satisfy existing evoked goals" (March, 1997, p. 12). This trap leads to quick, simplified solutions and reifies social tropes of inequity. "If we aren't aware of our discourse, understanding, and the moves we are making, we are liable to reinforce the system we seek to dismantle" (Safir & Dugan, 2021, p. 44). Leadership training, evaluation, and promotion traditions are rooted in these traps and tropes; CLE principles and processes provide an antidote.

CLEs invite community members to offer their assets and engage in root cause analysis to encourage innovative ideas and local wisdom to address change efforts. CLEs are democratic spaces in which traditionally marginalized voices are heard, people and place are valued, and trust is strong enough to address conflict. We believe a crucial starting point for successful CLE implementation includes gracious space tenets we identified in Chapter 2.

Gracious space has purchase with the educational leaders and teachers with whom we work. Students and colleagues create gracious spaces in their work settings and meetings to establish trust and create effective learning spaces. When we first introduce gracious space with a group, we explore the four elements—spirit, setting, inviting the stranger, and learning in public—through a creative process. In one successful process, we divide into groups, and each group develops a short skit to demonstrate one gracious space element to the group [Tools 2B and 2C].

In addition, we practice gracious space through dynamic mindfulness as a regular practice in meetings and classrooms, focusing on arts integration as a cornerstone of our pedagogy and organizing meeting structures and agendas in ways that support active participation and sustained trust. As Lori Collins, a district leader in North Carolina, shared,

> The work of Community Learning Exchanges has dramatically impacted how I lead others. I set the tone to explore our environment as a gracious space. In many instances, we are strangers, whether based on our experience, understanding of the topic, or simply our lack of knowing each other. By using gracious space processes, teacher mentors invite beginning teachers to share experiences that support increased efficacy, build better relationships, and provide safe, equitable environments. I worked with high school students across our district and opened the CLE with the definition of gracious space. The students from diverse ethnic groups internalized the meaning of gracious space. Media centers became places where students—without judgment but with curiosity, humor, and acceptance shared inequities and biases that they had witnessed and/or experienced. During the closing circle, another CLE protocol, students expressed the experience in single words; they felt seen, heard, understood, and respected. I introduced gracious space as a church leader to establish an atmosphere in which youth and elders could share. To be relevant to today's youth, we must provide a setting for youth to feel loved and welcomed and elders' wisdom respected. In the gracious space youth were heard and elders acted as mentors.

CLEs are spaces in which, if we listen in dialogue with each and use our collective assets, we can address issues and foster an environment of possibility. To start, Table 3.2 is a game of Tic Tac Toe to investigate the CLE axioms and gracious space [Tool 3A]. In the next chapter, we highlight several additional protocols.

All formal and informal, synchronous and asynchronous, meetings are "exchanges." We provide a template agenda with outcomes, agreements, and specific learning activities. All WebExchanges as online synchronous meetings include outcomes, agreements, dynamic mindfulness, and personal narratives and small-group activities, culturally responsive pedagogies, and a reflective debrief. As we discussed in Chapter 2, while we urge readers to adapt, we caution that our experience and research findings indicate that three criteria are of utmost importance in an agenda—creating a throughline from start to finish, centering through dynamic mindfulness, and using personal narratives as a routine practice (see Table 3.3; [Tool 3B]). Every choice for the agenda is a part of the throughline. The facilitator's critical role is to remain true to the agenda components and provide the context and the glue from one experience to the next and support participants in connecting each experience to meeting outcomes.

Table 3.2. CLE Axioms and Gracious Space Tic Tac Toe

Directions: Take turns with a partner selecting a "square." Read the prompt aloud and briefly respond with a story or thought (1–2 minutes). The goal is not to mark three squares in a row but to listen attentively to your partner's story. However, let "three in a row" guide your choice of squares!		
Conversations Are Critical and Central Pedagogical Processes. At the core of social learning theory is the need to create gracious spaces and healthy relationships for participants to share their stories. Storytelling and conversation are mediating tools for relationships that exist at the core of the learning. CLE Axiom 2	*Learn in Public.* Learning in public requires humility, a willingness to explore assumptions and let go of the "right way" of doing things, and being willing to change one's mind. Be transparent and be willing to say you made a mistake or apologize. Gracious space has the potential to transform the human heart and entire groups or organizations.	*Hope and Change Are Built on Assets and Dreams of Locals and Their Communities.* When CLE participants tell their stories, they map their gifts, ideas, and hopes. The identification, construction, and naming of these assets invites CLE participants to view their lives, change efforts, and community in new ways. CLE Axiom 5
Setting A gracious space appeals to the five senses and invites a spirit of the 6th sense of intuition, creativity, and imagination. Paying attention to simple hospitality (food, drink) and items that reflect your energy and personality, or goals for work (visual) creates a unique gracious space.	*Learning and Leadership Are a Dynamic Social Process.* Learning how to lead and learn within the context of relationships is at the core of leadership and the construction of the necessary conditions that nurture this development in an inviting and dignified manner. CLE Axiom 1	*Spirit* Bringing the spirit of **Gracious Space** to any place means that, as individuals and a collective, we invite and welcome each other to fully participate. We exude compassion, joy, hope, curiosity, and humor. When we bring these elements into relationships and collective spaces, we are "being" and enacting gracious space.
Crossing Boundaries Enriches the Development and Educational Process. The willingness and ability to experience a world outside our daily comfort zone is necessary to break the isolation of people, organizations, and communities. The boundary crossing can include borders of geography, economic standing, age, culture and race, gender, faith, and personal abilities. CLE Axiom 4	*Connect with the Stranger/ Invite the Stranger.* Borrowed from Parker Palmer (1983), the term "stranger" refers to any individual who is not typically involved in the conversation. Inviting the stranger often means opening up to include a new idea or perspective. We need the stranger inside us and ideas from others—and it's good to remember that we and our ideas are often strange to someone else.	*The People Closest to the Issues Are Best Situated to Discover Answers to Local Concerns.* CLEs organize around specific topics, and participants share their individual and community stories, experiences, and strategies around those topics. Such engagement fosters a creative agency that helps people find their power and voice. CLE Axiom 3

Table 3.3. Sample CLE Agenda

Outcomes (Use observable action verbs)	Agreements
1. Cultivate relational trust and commit to supporting one another. 2. Gain an understanding of gracious space and CLE axioms. 3. Engage in an asset mapping process. 4. Practice useful and transferable strategies to engage in necessary conversations within and across communities.	• Be patient with each other. • Speak your truth to your level of comfort. • Support equitable dialogue. • Take risks in engaging in conversations.

Time Min.	Activity 90-Minute Meeting	Choose Facilitator List Artifact
10	**Welcome and Overview**	
	Dynamic mindfulness	
10	**Personal Narrative** How does this image speak to you about an asset you possess in working in groups?	Note: Choose an image. https://www.rlmartstudio.com/ Share in pairs.
15	Tic Tac Toe: Community Learning Exchange Axioms and Gracious Space	Pairs
10	Asset-Framing by Trabian Shorters Read and highlight	Teams of four
20	Asset Mapping Posters	Teams of four
15	Gallery Walk and Comments *Sharing Cross Site Learning*	Individuals look at other posters and leave notes
10	Closing Reflection *Sticky Note Activity*	

CONCLUSION

Community as text provides an innovative, democratic, and engaging necessity for engaging in the critical work of continuous improvement in schools and districts. Our success is neither a secret nor a recipe. We make our processes public and transparent so others can emulate, adapt, and improve our ideas and protocols—real, meaningful change needs to come from within, and the rationale behind community as text provides an anchor. Our work is predicated on inviting, welcoming, enticing, exciting, and engaging voices. However, taking on this work requires courage to be vulnerable. As Brené Brown (2021) says, "Vulnerability is not winning or losing;

it's having the courage to show up and be seen when we have no control over the outcome."

We support a marked shift from the traditions of a leadership hierarchy to a collective style of leadership (Benham & Cooper, 2000). In such a model, the organizational actors are mutually connected by the enterprise of the organization; they share in the successes and are collectively engaged in problem solving (Wenger, 1998). The work starts with narratives, a conversation for hope grounded in ancestral roots. We learn when we hear, witness, engage, and reflect—when we make meaning from our practice—what Argyris and Schön (1996) call double-loop learning, a learning that accommodates better practice. This takes a certain kind of vulnerability and courage—the vulnerability to learn from one another, witness each other's stories, and support inclusive communities and the courage to take intentional actions to interrupt the systemsworld by privileging our lifeworlds into the process (Sergiovanni, 2000).

Community Learning Exchanges are designed to authorize the voices of insiders while we still listen to valuable and helpful external voices from the research and practice. The community as text processes helps us rebuke the traditional social contract of trusting the system—what Hobbes calls the "Leviathan." Community as text is a new social contract in which the people and the context where constituents live and work underscore a moral obligation to be activists and engage in civil disobedience in oppressive systems. The *wisdom of people* and *power of place* help us "rehabilitate the dominant narrative" (Guajardo et al., 2016, p. 15). In CLEs, we learn the value of being uncertain and sharing ideas with others until we can jointly figure out a course of action (Jackson, 2023). In the next chapter, we provide vivid examples of the ways we can actively become inquirers and practitioner-researchers of our work by mapping our school and community contexts and attending to the tenets of participatory activist research and liberatory design.

Resources and Tools for Chapter 3

https://www.tcpress.com/filebin/PDFs/9780807786147_supp.pdf
(See page 7 for a QR code linking to this URL.)
3A. Gracious Space & CLE: Tic-Tac-Toe
3B. Effective Agendas

Part II

CHANGES IN PRACTICE

CHAPTER 4

Practitioner-Research in Action

> Through the participatory action and activist research project, I built my skills as a facilitator, coach, and researcher in order to transform the school culture, one step at a time, by creating better, joyful learning experiences for Chinese ELLs.
>
> (Lau-Yee, 2023, p. 196)

Ideally, an educational professional is a lifelong learner who values uncertainty, curiosity, and excellence as attributes that support continuous improvement processes—for self, colleagues, and the institutions in which we work. While adult professional learning is often associated with formal events using CLE processes, adult learners also learn *in situ*—on the job and in informal ways. As discussed in Chapter 2, effective adult learning includes the necessary conditions for cultivating and sustaining relational trust. In Chapter 7, we highlight variables that support transfer to practice—attending to emotional support, engaging in experiential learning, and becoming ambassadors for change with colleagues. In this chapter, we focus on how leaders and teachers become practitioner-researchers by using readily available evidence. In offering stories of relationships and collaborative work that influence and bind our work as professionals, we solidify the community as text by offering concrete school and community mapping protocols.

For school and district leaders to become practitioner-researchers, they need a roadmap that extends beyond normative statements about what to do. To provide that roadmap, we begin by defining "practitioner-researcher" and identify inquiry practices that support them in the role of lead practitioner-researcher: (1) Community Learning Exchange protocols as a method for mapping and collecting evidence, (2) participatory action and activist research principles and tools, and (3) liberatory design principles, modes, and mindsets.

LEADERS AND TEACHERS AS PRACTITIONER-RESEARCHERS

Practitioner-researchers have a collective approach to data analysis and decision-making. The practitioner-researcher emphasizes the importance of a practitioner who learns how to use qualitative research tools. As we concentrate on how leaders work with teachers, the same principles and practices apply to working with families, community members, and organizations. As inquiry-minded practitioner-researchers, school and district leaders act in concert with teachers as practitioner-researchers to reimagine practical ways of approaching accountability for achieving equitable student learning results. By engaging in data construction and analyzing available data as a source of evidence, they can transform teaching and learning for adult learners who, in turn, influence equitable student outcomes. In other words, leaders who work collaboratively with teachers and district leaders are diagnosticians and designers (Spillane & Coldren, 2011). As practitioner-researchers engage in cycles of inquiry using real-time data to make decisions about incremental changes, they use evidence and equity-based tools to change systems and structures. Every position in the hierarchy—district, principal, coach, or teacher—can support student learning and develop their capacities as practitioner-researchers (Figure 4.1).

To effectively grow systems that result in just outcomes, schools need school and district leaders who:

- support others to inquire about practices and cultivate the dispositions of uncertainty and experimentation (Jackson, 2023; Snowden & Boone, 2007).
- support constructivist developmental adult learning through active sensemaking and sensegiving (Drago-Severson et al. 2023; Norris, 2022).
- use protocols and tools to co-construct and analyze the abundant daily "street" data that inform collective decisions (hunter et al., 2003; Safir & Dugan, 2020; Tredway & Militello, 2024).

In our work with leaders, becoming practitioner-researchers is attainable and inclusive of all the constituents (students, families, school leaders, district leaders, and teachers) and places (schools, districts, and community). Initially, a school or district leader works with others who become co-practitioner-researchers (CPRs). A school leader must be engaged in two levels of sensemaking and sensegiving (Norris, 2022). First, leaders make sense of their understanding and share their sensemaking or understanding with others. Then, they engage community members in collective sensemaking and sensegiving. Thus, the leader occupies a linchpin role in the process of change (Theoharis, 2024) as facilitator and co-learner.

Figure 4.1. Leadership Chain of Effect on Student Learning

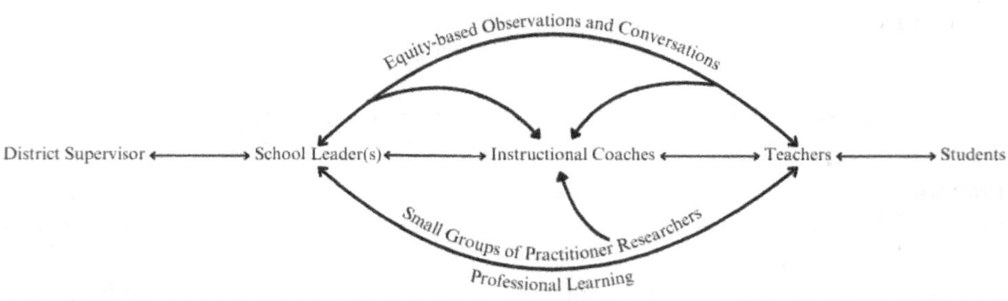

To reimagine their roles as researchers of their work, we utilize frameworks as guides to engage in data construction and analysis. A key characteristic of useful data construction as opposed to data collection, which has the tone of data extraction, is using research-embedded tools—instructional tools that "educators (and others) . . . use to carry out their everyday work" (Bohannon et al., 2024, p. 13). In other words, use tools that help teachers and leaders make visible their daily work and evidence. For Bohannon et al. (2024), these data sources are hidden in plain sight. Particularly important in the data construction process is using tools—protocols or processes—that mediate learning of teachers and leaders (Wise & Jacobi, 2010; Woo & Hendriksen, 2023) and underscore the importance of continuous improvement and coherence (Yurkofsky et al., 2020).

As we urge practitioners to take on roles as researchers, we offer participatory action and activist research (PAAR) methods. Leaders with teachers can use data in plain sight—for example, classroom observations and meeting artifacts from using Community Learning Exchange tools. These processes and tools support educators to use real time data as they collectively focus on equity and honor the wisdom of the place and people. Leaders with small groups of teachers or district leaders with groups of principals can and should use these types of evidence to make decisions. In this chapter, we go beyond normative "should" statements by providing specific tools—grounded in theory and useful for practice—that have supported our work and the work of leaders and teachers.

Because the overuse of frameworks and underuse of specific processes present a danger in our work, our stories relay a narrative of how we have melded three approaches—Community Learning Exchanges (CLEs), participatory action and activist research, and liberatory design. Over years of teaching, leading, and working with colleagues and practitioners in leadership preparation programs, grant-funded projects, and EdD programs, we have designed and adapted shared practices. In this chapter, we fortify the use of CLE principles by identifying tools we co-developed and continue to refine. We recognize that the context is complex as there are multiple contexts to consider. The byword here is adaptation to your context, not fidelity to a tool—quick, solution-driven approaches are a leadership trap. The right tools can support leaders and teachers to mine daily data as a means of building evidence (data construction) to make decisions that reinforce iterative and hopefully enduring change efforts.

COMMUNITY LEARNING EXCHANGE PEDAGOGY AND PROTOCOLS

The genesis of the CLE approach we discussed partially in Chapter 3 is important to our development as professionals. An event in 2011 shaped the future of our work. The CLE team hosted a thought leaders meeting at Highlander Center—the civil rights and education center where Miles Horton and his frequent guest, Paolo Freire, had conversations and Rosa Parks and Martin Luther King Jr. worked with Septima Clarke in the early 1950s to practice nonviolent civil disobedience.

By 2020, the CLE group had written a book and hosted two American Education Research Association (AERA) sessions on CLE principles as a research methodology. Matt and Lynda started an EdD program at East Carolina, hosted local and national Community Learning Exchanges, and secured a USDOE grant—Project I^4—to implement the theory and processes with school leaders across the country.

As we analyzed our work with leaders and teachers, we identified inquiry practices that emanated from CLEs, and we understood how activist research and liberatory design were consistent with our values and beliefs of dialogical education, critical pedagogy, and community. To augment our thinking, we needed a trusted colleague to bring an outside heart, learning, eye, and ear to our thinking. Joe Flessa, associate dean at Ontario Institute of Education (OISE) and a colleague, is such a person.

As discussed in Chapter 3, Community Learning Exchanges are often events. But foundational to the events are the axioms that represent standards for operationalizing values in formal and informal interactions and processes. While we have hosted multiday CLEs, CLE processes are implicit in meeting agendas and the informal interactions that adults have with each other in school and community contexts. To cultivate trust as a necessary condition for change, agendas support centering through dynamic mindfulness and storytelling using personal narratives. Tools support collaborative dialogue and yield evidence for practitioner-researchers to make school and district decisions. In particular in this chapter, we reference tools we use to engage in the community as text, including community mapping and tools for uncovering the assets and challenges of a school or district community.

School and Community Mapping

Because schools and districts are complex environments with multiple layers of formal and informal systems and structures—representing, in many cases, different views of the same general context—mapping supports us to engage community members in uncovering assets and tracking formal and informal lines of decision-making and power. With an understanding of existing systems and structures, the school or district community can better reinforce a collaborative leadership culture in which leaders make decisions using inclusive, transparent, and equitable democratic processes and the data they collect and analyze.

Paying attention to the abundant resources in schools or districts is critical; instead of jumping too quickly to a needs assessment, which emphasizes challenges and problems, we remember that the people closest to the work are best situated to discover answers to local concerns (Guajardo et al., 2016). Concentrating on the resources at hand—our individual and collective assets—is the best way to address the issues at hand. The assets include knowledge and skills of individuals and groups, productive organizational structures, use of time, and relational trust between and among the people in the school: parents, students, teachers, support staff, partners, community members, and administrators.

Community mapping offers one inquiry method that situates learning in the context of the lived realities and assets of people in schools and communities (Tredway, 1999). By increasing interactions between the people in schools and districts and the primary constituents—students and families (Tredway, 2003; Tindle et al., 2005)—they together learn the history of a community and "remove cultural barriers and unearth sociocultural assets and natural resources" (Ordoñez-Jasis & Myck-Wayne, 2012, p. 31). For example, in a 3-day Community Learning Exchange in northeast North Carolina at a former plantation that had once been a Black school and was now a conference center, 80 persons engaged in historical community mapping. The CLE theme was the West African concept of *Sankofa*, meaning to go forward, we must look back. Four local facilitators worked with experienced CLE facilitators to design historical community mapping in four communities: Rocky Mount, *Community Rebirth*; Halifax, *Historic Downtown*; Williamston, *Civil Rights Movement*; and Oxford, *Remnants of an Unresolved Murder*. Working with a school principal to design a community mapping of Rocky Mount, the group visited a historic community theater located on the "Black" side of the railroad tracks, a Thelonious Monk mural, a local mortuary, new Black-owned businesses, and the high school where Martin Luther King delivered a practice "I Have a Dream" speech in spring 1963. Reconvening at the conference center, the four groups shared experiences and discussed organizing similar CLEs in their contexts.

In another example in a Pittsburgh community, we worked with Duquesne University colleagues to support a story-mapping process. Based on the West African community griot—the community storyteller—the process exemplifies how groups or teams can become community researchers of assets in local communities. Small teams collected stories of community residents and advocates, wrote and analyzed the stories in small groups, and designed performance pieces based on the stories (Tredway & Generett, 2015).

In another example, a group of Georgia principals drew maps of their schools to glean information from using their schools as a text. As they mapped readily available evidence, they better understood assets and potential issues. In using this mapping process, one principal better understood the schoolwide focus on project-based learning in STEM. In identifying how science and math teams cultivated possibilities, she could think about programmatic additions to support their efforts (Figure 4.2).

Another principal said, "We too often start with obstacles, but we need to start with community assets. I don't look at obstacles as being a threat; I look at difficult circumstances as being opportunities. I am always looking for that silver lining in every sort of situation."

Based on these examples, participants may focus on understanding a specific issue or event by naming physical and social capital assets. The mapping process depends on building a strong rapport with community members by listening to their stories and what they believe to be important about their community. Only then can the mapping organizers identify community leaders who can become community advocates. As community residents analyze maps with each other and engage in

Figure 4.2. Mapping the Assets of the School's STEM Programs

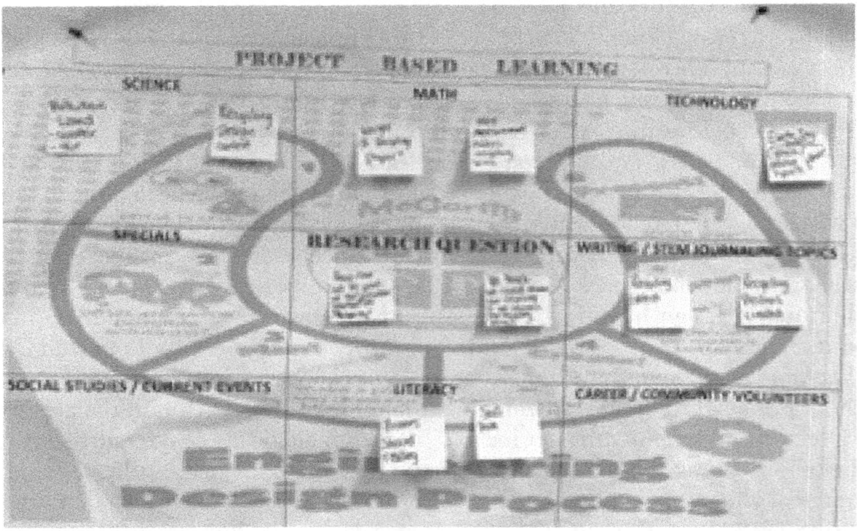

Courtesy of Karla Dodgen.

planning, leaders seek solutions with the very people responsible for improvements. As they map the assets and challenges, they can work together to understand the context to ready themselves for action [Tool 4A].

Immersive Site Visits

Place-based learning in visits to community sites can be useful to all constituents if the visit moves beyond a "show and tell" experience. Community or school site visits can take multiple forms but should be designed to encourage reciprocity and be sufficiently immersive to gain a deep understanding of place. The visitors need roles and responsibilities with clear protocols and processes to interact in the community spaces in ways that foster gracious space and achieve learning outcomes.

In a CLE at Gallaudet University in Washington, DC, we focused on effective special education practices. Using CLE protocols, participants chose one of five immersive site locations that supported advocacy for persons with disabilities: Gallaudet campus and museums, Capital City Public Charter School, Latin American Youth Center, Autistic Self-Advocacy Network at National Youth Transitions Center 5, and Adaptive Services Division of MLK Public Library. A facilitator worked with each site coordinator to co-construct an interactive and informative experience in which the participants had tools for collecting data and analyzing evidence. Starting with an essential question, they incorporated CLE pedagogical elements; at each site visit, participants connected the site visit to their work in their school or organization. In reconvening, participants from all site visits shared with other CLE participants.

Processes for Uncovering Community Assets and Challenges

The untapped assets of a school or community's history, experiences, and present realities offer assets to school or district change efforts and should be the first step in any inquiry process.

As a result, participants articulate current challenges while they rely on collective assets to address an issue. PhotoVoice [Tool 4B] and Digihunt [Toll 4C] offer methods for gathering data to name assets and challenges, and the fishbone analysis is a graphic representation of the assets and challenges related to a specific inquiry or issue. The processes build rapport and relational trust among the practitioner-researchers who collaboratively collect and analyze school or district data.

PhotoVoice

PhotoVoice is an interactive protocol in which participants gather and caption images as evidence about a concept, topic, or question. PhotoVoice encourages participants to lead a research process as they visually represent and narrate their everyday experiences (Foster-Fishman et al., 2005). PhotoVoice encourages participants (Wang et al., 1996) to draw upon their personal histories and experiences to tell their stories. Practitioner-researchers use this practice as a medium of knowledge transfer to inform leaders or policymakers instead of being told what to do (McIntyre, 2005). This level of openness supports increased responsiveness to the participants' identified needs and a means of discovering new possibilities for approaching change.

For example, a principal new to a school asked 12 teacher participants to collect photos and caption them to represent the school's core values. Then, groups of teachers engaged in conversations and summarized the essence of each photo in a word or phrase. One group synthesized words into an equation:

school culture = play and risk + growth and change + collaboration and community

Even though the principal had 20 years of experience, he had to understand anew the importance of creating the conditions for teachers to feel safe within the social culture (Palmer, 2021). Understanding school assets reminded the school leader that he needed to adjust his pace to build relationships and ensure that teachers were ready to take risks [Tool 4B].

DigiHunt

DigiHunt, a digital scavenger hunt, is an inquiry process using digital tools to make meaning about an identified question or issue [Tool 4C]. The facilitator develops an overarching question and specific questions related to a place (school or community) or inquiry question. Small groups collect information to respond to questions, usually by taking phone photos or interviewing people they encounter. Similar to PhotoVoice, the participants caption the images. Then groups share the information with the facilitator, who develops a visual gallery and/or source folder so that participants can analyze the images or digital documents and develop a collective understanding in response to the overarching question.

At a San Marcos, Texas CLE, a colleague organized a DigiHunt to document the city's political history. The facilitator developed specific directions (e.g., take a photo that represents the Mexican American contributions to the city), which responded to the question about understanding the city's political history. Each group forwarded digital photo images to the facilitator, who organized the images from multiple groups in a slide show. Groups reconvened to analyze the images and develop a response to the overarching question.

In another example, a group met twice to address a critical question of school power dynamics: How democratic and collaborative are we? The specific questions on which groups collected documents or images included: (1) What does leadership look like? (2) How do decisions get made? (3) What does conflict look like? Where and when does it take place? and (4) Where is formal and informal power situated? Participants collected digital sources and documents and shared them with the facilitator. They analyzed the collective evidence at the second meeting to respond to the questions. The process led to a re-examination of the school's commitment to democratic structures for adults. Using tools that increase equitable participation, a group used readily available evidence from the school to address a key issue of local concern.

Graphic Representation of Assets and Challenges

To use mapping to identify assets and challenges, the fishbone provides a useful graphic organizer. Because we depend on using assets to address challenges, Rosenthal (2019) modified the original fishbone analysis activity (Bryk et al., 2015) to include assets and challenges at three levels: micro (school), meso (district), and macro (structural). Figure 4.3 represents an example from an EdD study (Garcia, 2021); the same process can be used for shorter-term efforts to address school or district change. When a group decides to address a dilemma or issue in their context, they should name and analyze the assets as well as the challenges.

The processes related to mapping and analyzing assets and challenges represent a sampling of how we convert CLE principles or axioms to doable pedagogical practices. As a result, the tools fortify change efforts and ground school or district organizational actors in becoming practitioner-researchers. To fully engage, however, they need to learn skills related to participatory action and activist research methods. While school-based inquirers do not need an in-depth understanding of research methodology, they do need a set of practices that they can use to act and fulfill the social justice imperative of activist research.

Participatory Action and Activist Research (PAAR) Principles and Practices

Participatory action and activist research (PAAR) supports our commitment to inquiry *by* and *with* practitioners as researchers (Hale, 2008; Kemmis et al., 2014). We used PAAR theory and methods in our work with 77 EdD students and 216

Figure 4.3. Fishbone of Assets and Challenges

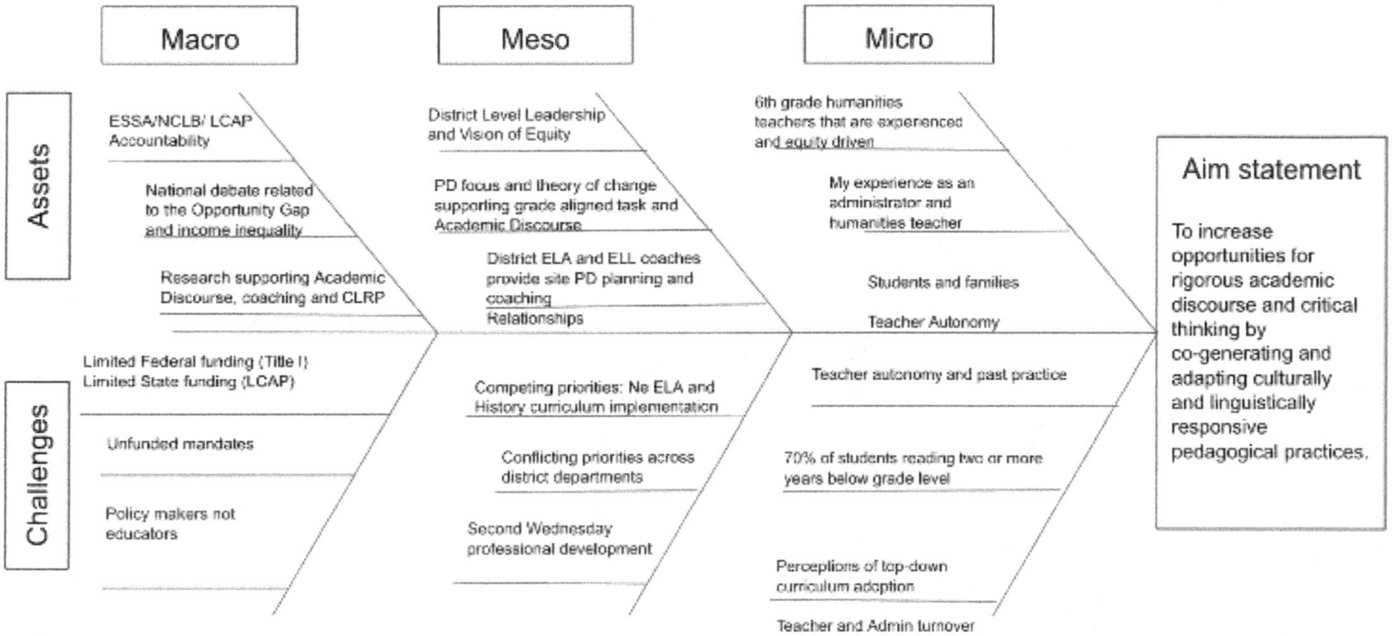

Courtesy of Marcos M. Garcia.

school leaders in a U.S. Department of Education (USDOE)–funded project to support school leaders. Starting the EdD program, we needed a consistent and coherent approach to research methodology. In participatory action research, "the focus is on personally and collectively enacting the changes we want to see on a day-to-day basis, even if such efforts are messy and imperfect" (hunter et al., 2013, p. 2). Practitioner-researchers learn to code and analyze oral, written, and visual forms data that offer evidence about puzzling issues they identify in their contexts (Saldaña, 2016).

In the work with the school leaders in the grant-funded project to address math instruction, we used equity-centered network improvement communities (EC-NICs) with small groups of teachers. We agree with Herr and Anderson (2014) that "inquiry that is done *by* or *with* insiders in an organization or community, but never *to* or *on* them. . . . [which] makes action central to the research enterprise" (p. 3, italics in original) and supports activities (cycles of inquiry). Yet we chose participatory action and activist research because activist research comports with CLE axioms and liberatory design principles (see Figure 4.4 for a comparison of CLEs, activist research, and liberatory design). The social justice emphasis of activist research practices is intrinsic to liberatory design—beyond the typical design thinking process, the goal of liberatory design thinking is (1) to analyze the ways racism and inequity are "baked into" systems and (2) to ensure the meaningful participation of those most affected by the design and implementation decisions.

Actions of PAAR Practitioner-Researchers

In participatory action and activist research (PAAR), practitioners as researchers focus on a change related to a social justice issue. Kemmis et al. (2014) term this

Figure 4.4. Modes of Liberatory Design

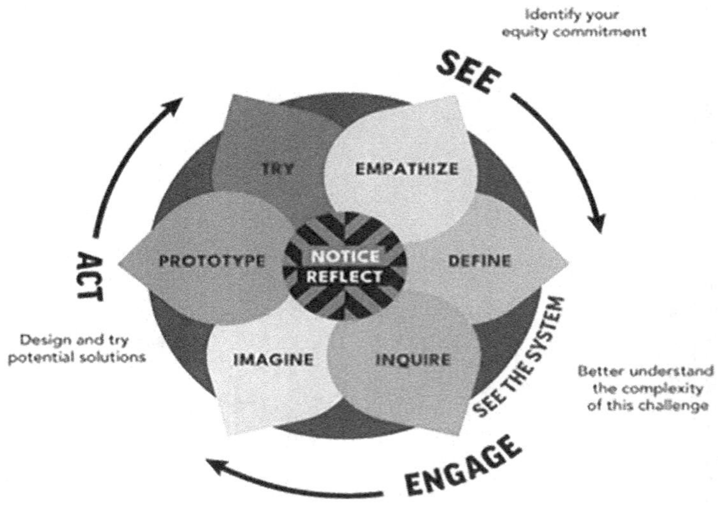

Courtesy of the National Equity Project.

critical research; the goal is to "critique and challenge, to transform, and to analyze power relationships" (Merriam & Tisdell, 2015, p. 59). The responsibility of activist practitioner-researchers is to fully engage a collective group (those closest to the work) in enacting short and informative cycles of inquiry and using iterative evidence to adjust the processes based on iterative evidence.

The PAAR process has the potential to authorize collaborative spaces within schools. PAAR provides a research design, but at times, the issues and identified improvement areas were rooted in deficit-thinking traps (Valencia, 2010; McKenzie & Scheurich, 2004). Thus, we converted the problem of practice to focus of practice (FoP); using a theory action to analyze the situation, practitioner-researchers can determine leverage points for greater efforts and use the PAAR processes to collect data and maintain an equity focus. We documented school-level use of tools (Chapter 5) and processes (Chapters 6 and 7) that exemplify how the PAAR process can become the essential daily work of teachers and school and district leaders.

Data Construction and Analysis Processes

The term "data" often has a negative connotation that causes teachers and leaders to cringe. However, data as daily evidence—street data (Safir & Dugan, 2021) or pragmatic data (Cobb et al., 2018)—is useful for practitioner-researchers as they make collaborative decisions about instructional practices or other change efforts in a school or district. In describing concrete interactive methods for data construction and analysis, activist practitioner-researchers recognize the utility of using data as a means of having specific information or evidence to make informed decisions.

School and district leaders used the PAAR process in their dissertation work (see Appendix A for full list of dissertations). In addition, in Project I[4]—the USDOE-funded implementation and research effort—principals used improvement science practices fortified with CLE axioms and pedagogies and activist research principles to engage in change efforts with small groups of teachers. Using processes to understand self and context, they collected and analyzed evidence (see Chapter 5) and engaged in meaningful conversations (Chapter 6) and professional learning (Chapter 7). They consistently used probes or experiments with small groups of teachers before expanding to a larger context. Several stories exemplify how school and district leaders worked with small groups who became ambassadors of change efforts.

A district principal supervisor worked with four elementary principals in a co-practitioner-researcher (CPR) group for 15 months. Group members wanted to strengthen their understanding and enactment of culturally responsive school leadership (CRSL). By creating a trusting space for leaders by using personal narratives plus reading about CRSL, the group examined personal identities, fortified themselves in a trusted group, shared dilemmas of practice, and enacted CRSL in their schools. Using the critical friends consultation protocols to bring dilemmas of practice to the group, Tang (2023), the district supervisor, said "the brave space we had in our meetings was vital for them to practice in private; these kinds of brave spaces for leaders are pivotal for sustaining change" (p. 155). As the lead researcher adopted a new identity as a practitioner-researcher, he "developed a greater sensitivity in listening for sightings—words, demeanors, actions, and other indicators—and categorizing them to make meaning, thus informing my immediate or long-term leadership actions" (p. 154) and engaged the four principals as co-practitioner-researchers in using data from their schools to make decisions.

In several school-based projects, the lead practitioner-researcher worked with small groups of teachers or leaders using activist research principles and CLE axioms and processes to shift teacher practices over three cycles of inquiry:

- A coordinator worked with three teachers to fully integrate the arts into elementary classroom content. As the teachers kept art journals and committed to practicing art, they reimagined themselves as teachers who nurtured creative mindsets and fully integrated the arts in their classrooms (Ledo-Lane, 2023).
- A principal organized an in-house teacher induction program to support new teachers in becoming culturally responsive educators. In monthly meetings, novice teachers discussed their values about teaching and learning. The principal conducted regular observations and conversations with individual teachers. The group processes supported them in becoming more confident and effective teachers (Lassiter, 2023).
- A district administrator supported four principals at schools identified as not fully serving Black students; they co-developed practices for shifting practices and determined that "culturally responsive leaders need a brave space with outside facilitation in order to authentically reflect on their power and privilege and build racial literacy, take risks, and make sustainable change" (Quadros-Meis, 2021, p. i).

Over time, participatory action activist research processes help develop leaders to cultivate relational trust, engage a small group of leaders or teachers to collectively address dilemmas of practice, raise questions of inequity, and decide on antiracist responses. To further enhance their capacities as practitioner-researchers, the liberatory design process—in tandem with Community Learning Exchanges and activist research—strengthens the capacity of the practitioner-researchers to effectively address change efforts.

LIBERATORY DESIGN: MODES, MINDSETS, AND ACTIONS

As long-time collaborators with the National Equity Project (NEP), their design thinking and change theory approach matches our principles and practices. NEP partnered with the Stanford D-school to develop liberatory design principles (Anaissie et al., 2021; Blignaut, 2019; Cary, 2018; Snowden & Boone, 2007) that support addressing complex school and district issues and forward a set of underlying questions about how race, class, and oppression affect schools and districts. These distinctions are critical. In chemistry, solutions are relatively simple combinations with predictable

Table 4.1. Frames for Supporting Practitioner-Researchers in Schools and Districts

A fundamental principle for supporting practitioner-researchers is the goal of social change. All frames support the importance of cultivating the necessary conditions for engaging practitioner researchers in trusting relationships, "a contingent and negotiated feature of professional or social engagement with others" (Sachs, p. 83). In integrating the three theories and protocols from the three frames, researcher practitioners can use evidence to make collaborative decisions in schools and districts.

Community Learning Exchange (CLE) Axioms	Activist Research (AR) Principles	Liberatory Design (LD): Principles, Modes, and Mindsets
Learning and leadership are dynamic social processes.	AR is participatory social process that aims to transform theory and practice.	In dynamic social environments that do not have immediate solutions, PRs embrace complexity and use a flexible and experimental approach to problem solving instead of relying on established methods.
Conversations are critical and central pedagogical processes.	Because AR is iterative and generative, dialogical and reciprocal learning among all the participants is crucial as "professionals generate and sustain the energy for change within their evolving relationships."	Teams engage in "seeing" the systems of racism and inequity by empathizing, defining, and inquiring in teams before acting. The team members work through fear and discomfort to recognize oppressive systems or practices by staying engaged in dialogue.
The people closest to the issues are best situated to discover answers to local concerns.	Inclusiveness, collective action, and recognition of different types of expertise inform actions. AR relies on autonomy to those most affected by specific programs or policies. Critical reflection (praxis) is necessary for decision-making.	The team members engaged in the change effort seek liberatory collaboration, practice self-awareness, and imagine/reimagine and design a prototype for experimenting or trying out possible ways to approach the issue.
Crossing boundaries enriches development and the educational processes.	Renegotiating power relationships to privilege local and culturally appropriate ways of knowing is central, collaborative, and emancipatory.	In seeing the system as oppressive and deciding about initial change efforts, team members exercise creative courage and act to transform power structures.
Hopes and change are built on assets and dreams of locals and their communities.	The primary validity is the usefulness to participants as they maintain focus on social justice goals of equity and excellence.	As team members notice and reflect throughout the entire process of seeing, engaging, and acting, they attend to healing and keep focused on the group assets and possibilities.

results, but emulsions depend on complex factors—some clear and others not so obvious. Relationships between cause and effect can usually be discerned in complicated systems because the problem is compartmentalized. For example, implementing a new curriculum is a complicated problem, but leaders can rely on past experience and predictable steps to facilitate satisfactory implementation. In complex systems, cause-and-effect relations are not immediately clear, and outcomes are difficult to predict because the system has interconnected parts—often with undercurrents that have never been addressed, not just the individual components. School culture, for instance, emerges from the complex interactions of students, parents, teachers, and school leaders. Therefore, when addressing problems in a complex adaptive system, a flexible and experimental approach focused on social justice approaches to problem solving is the best choice. In liberatory design, the theory, processes, and schematics of the NEP offer publicly available resources that support an equity-driven design and implementation process.

Thus, liberatory design (LD) is a good match with CLE axioms and PAAR methodology because all are directed at shifting relationships between those who hold power and those most impacted by change efforts. LD, CLE, and PAAR activities generate critical learning and increased agency for those closest to the work. Leaders who apply liberatory design principles with an equity perspective—empathy, team co-design, problem defining, prototyping and testing, reflection, and iteration—design and experiment with workable innovations to address complex equity challenges. Leaders and teachers who become researchers use liberatory design modes and mindsets to keep them focused on equity analysis and actions.

Modes

The liberatory design thinking modes offer an approach to an equity challenge (NEP, 2021). The three modes of liberatory design actions—See, Engage, and Act + Notice and Reflect—seem relatively simple on the surface but complex in enactment (Figure 4.5). Similar to the improvement science process of plan-do-study-act (PDSA), experimentation—prototyping and trying—is critical (Bryk et al., 2015). However, the improvement science "plan and do" does not necessarily consider the two essential elements before planning and acting—identifying the equity commitment, "seeing" the system of inequities, and understanding the complexity of the challenge before imagining. Second, in using the liberatory design process, prototyping from the design thinking processes (Nash, 2019) fortified with equity mindsets is another crucial and often missed step in the change process.

Two junctures in the LD process are critical—participants (1) collect and analyze evidence from stories of participants to understand their hopes and dreams and (2) gather evidence from the prototyping to determine the next steps for more trials or expanding efforts to a larger context. The LD process comports with PAAR emphasis on iterative and evidence-based cycles of inquiry. Concurrently, participants choose the most appropriate LD mindset for acting.

Mindsets

A liberatory design mindset—a habit of mind formed from experience—is similar to a growth mindset (Dweck, 2007) but includes critical mindsets related to equity and social justice. If the school or district organizational actors want to simultaneously interrupt inequities but have to work in an inequitable system, they need more than a growth mindset. Equity efforts often fail because of surface responses "as opposed to interrogating deeper causes produced by systemic oppression" (Anaissie et al., 2021, p. 1). Instead, developing the mindset of a co-conspirator (Love, 2019) offers concrete methods for those engaged in school or district change efforts to honor their values and make changes that respond to and fortify equity goals and outcomes. The 12 mindsets of NEP liberatory design are:

1. Build relational trust
2. Focus on human values
3. Work to transform power
4. Practice self-awareness
5. Seek liberatory collaboration
6. Exercise creative courage
7. Recognize oppression
8. Work with fear and discomfort
9. Take action to learn
10. Embrace complexity
11. Attend to healing
12. Share, don't sell

Liberatory Design in Action

In a PAAR project, an elementary school principal wanted to focus on revising the writing curriculum and understood the complexity of the challenge was a critical step. He used PhotoVoice to determine how teachers viewed the school and "I am from" emulation poems (Chapter 2) to understand and empathize with teachers about their hopes and dreams for the school. Teachers felt pride in the school and sought professional and personal growth. The principal, new to the school, recognized that he needed to involve a small group of teachers by experimenting with "safe-fail probes" to assess the intersections of teacher readiness to learn, his own skill set, and a "good recipe" for effective writing instruction (Palmer, 2021; Snowden & Boone, 2007). In other words, the principal said, "I learned that change in a complex system like a school is not linear and therefore requires an experimental approach" (Palmer, 2021, p. 154).

As shown in Figure 4.5, the principal used probes or experiments that had some purchase, but what made the difference was recognizing the moderate and strong possibilities that he determined through collecting and analyzing evidence (Palmer, 2021, p. 161). What might have been a likely idea—observations and

Figure 4.5. Connecting the Dots: Safe-Fail Probes Revealed the Strongest Possibility for Change

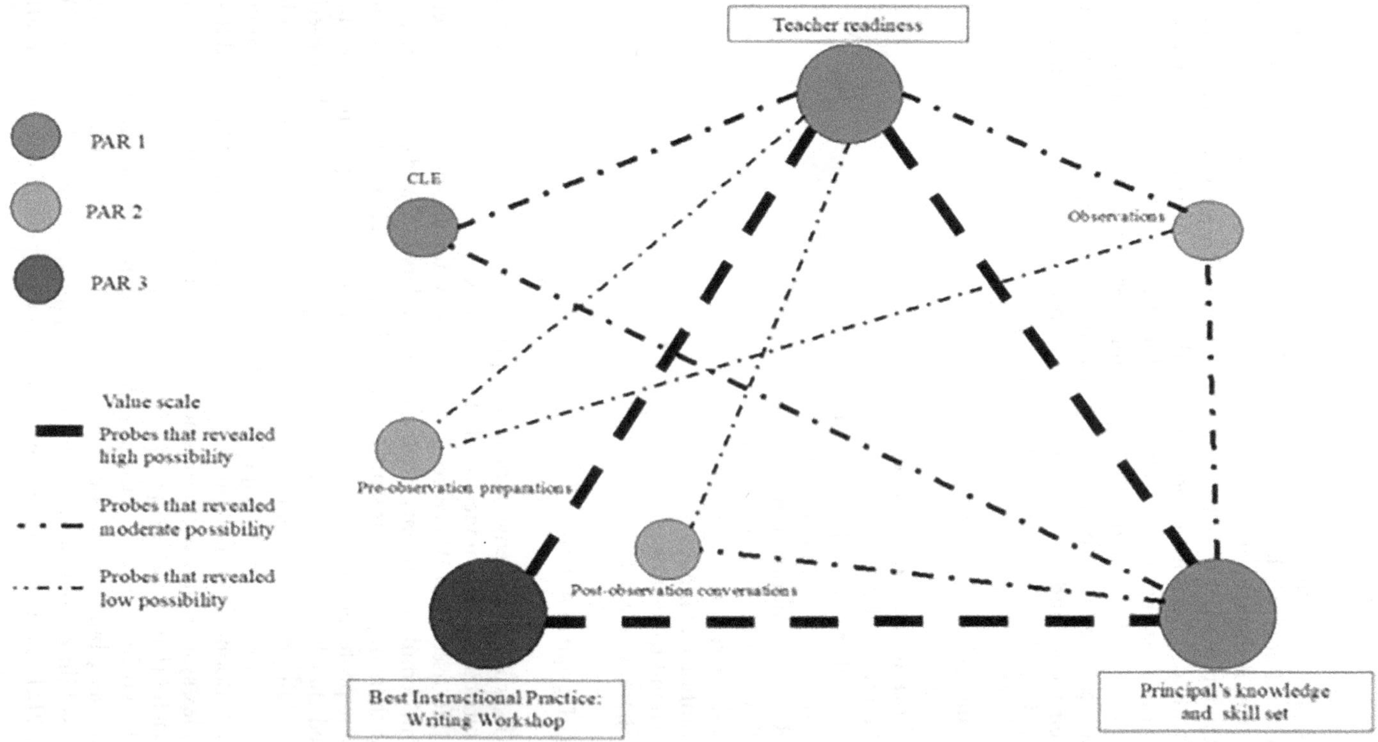

Courtesy of Michael Palmer.

conversations—did not work well in this context. Without the benefit of an LD process, he might have missed the possibility of the last probe—supporting a writing program with a small group of teachers who viewed writing as an equity issue and could act as anchors for use with the full staff.

CONCLUSION

The complex work of shifting teacher and leader practices requires intentional and systematic attention to each element outlined in earlier chapters and this chapter—the necessary conditions and the critical processes useful for change. This process is messy, iterative, and incremental (Gawande, 2017; hunter et al., 2013). Only through attention to the readiness of the adult learners, iterative processes of data construction and analysis, and use of the Community Learning Exchanges axioms and process, activist research methods, and liberatory design mode and mindsets can we hope to get inside the black boxes of classroom, school, and district change and slowly but surely see ways forward. By invigorating the possibility of shifts and engaging practitioners in using the daily data they have at their fingertips to make decisions, we hope to have a different way forward.

Resources and Tools for Chapter 4

https://www.tcpress.com/filebin/PDFs/9780807786147_supp.pdf
(See page 7 for a QR code linking to this URL.)

4A. Community Mapping: Asset Mapping
4B. Community Mapping: Asset Mapping PhotoVoice
4C. Community Mapping: Digihunt

CHAPTER 5

Evidence-Based Observations

One could argue that a time traveler from 100 years ago would be baffled by visiting an airport or driving a modern car, yet they would feel at home in a classroom. Schooling today still resembles images of Plato taking notes of Socrates' dialogues. In Cuban's (2023) book, *The Enduring Classroom*, he posits that schooling and classroom practices have remained stable—teacher-directed practices that are largely inequitable and at the low end of cognitive rigor. To support teacher practice as the primary target for change, principals need to assume roles as instructional leaders who support teacher growth (Mette et al., 2024). As Grissom et al. (2021) confirmed, principals are essential to school; they recommend four critical leadership actions: "Engaging in instructionally focused interactions with teachers; building a productive school climate; facilitating productive collaboration and professional learning communities; and managing personnel and resources strategically" (p. xv). The processes of observations, post-observation conversations, and professional learning are inextricably linked. In this chapter, we discuss how effective evidence-based observations lead to more effective conversations and professional learning (discussed in Chapters 6 and 7). In doing so, we offer one form of evidence-based data construction and analysis that supports leading and learning from within and can be a model for applying to other school level change. Unlike the autopsy data that is typical in school use, real-time data offer the leaders and teachers precise evidence of classroom practices—particularly inequitable classroom routines.

Without question, the school leader working in concert with teachers is the linchpin for improving student learning (Leithwood & Louis, 2012; Robinson et al., 2008). However, achieving this goal by being a culturally responsive leader of equity is crucial (Gooden et al., 2023; Khalifa, 2018; Leithwood et al., 2020). Too often, leaders get derailed from their commitments to equitable student learning because of time constraints or because the management role overtakes time and attention; in any case, school leaders do not fully assume the critical role of principal teacher and authentic instructional leader (Kafka, 2009; National Institute for Excellence in Teaching [NIET], 2021).

Beyond the time barrier, leaders need to diagnose appropriate, equitable, and effective teaching and communicate with teachers to examine and change ineffective practices. Novice leaders often enter the profession articulating the importance of equitable instructional leadership; however, they encounter barriers to actualizing their beliefs (Gooden & O'Doherty, 2015; O'Doherty & Ovando, 2013). Despite their beliefs, they form leadership habits that do not effectively expand student learning and shy away from the leadership actions that might motivate changes in teacher practices. Instead, they devote time to disciplinary or other management issues (Brill, 2008). We elevate key leadership actions that fortify the importance of the internal capacity of leaders and teachers as the leaders of change efforts. As several reports on district, school, and teacher leadership confirm, we need educational professionals at all levels to collaborate, engage, and build networks in schools and districts to build instructional capacity (Barnett, 2024; NIET, 2018, 2021).

We propose that school (and district) leaders become more effective instructional leaders of equitable and culturally responsive teaching practices by (1) fostering equitable and rigorous academic discourse in all classrooms, (2) gaining facility in using evidence-based observation tools as practitioner-researchers, and (3) supporting teachers through evidence-based conversations with teachers to change their practices. As they engage in data construction by observing and analyzing classroom practices and aggregating schoolwide evidence to have conversations with teachers, school leaders fulfill the Grissom et al. (2021) recommendations about engaging in instructionally focused interactions with teachers and facilitating productive collaboration and professional learning communities. As a result, leaders support teachers in developing a culture of peer observation and strategically managing other resources to support instructional shifts.

To accomplish these goals, leaders need to reimagine their use of time and cultivate teachers as allies in equitable and rigorous instruction (Mette et al., 2024). Often, principal days consist of brief and disconnected activities focused primarily on noninstructional tasks with limited attention to instruction (Hochbein et al., 2021). On average, elementary school principals spend 17 percent and high school principals spend 12.7 percent of their school day on instruction (Grissom et al., 2013). Undoubtedly, administrative tasks that benefit organizational coherency and contribute to the academic program are critical. However, to ensure the equitable student outcomes that abound in most school improvement plans, school leaders must invest targeted time and attention on effective instructional leadership. And their district supervisors should converse with the leaders about instruction and facilitate more useful principal professional learning (Goldring et al., 2020; Honig & Rainey, 2020; NIET, 2021).

In this chapter, we focus on critical sources for school improvement—real-time data rather than autopsy data, which is the typical focus of school improvement discussions. Data becomes useful evidence and information for school change only when school leaders, district supervisors, and teachers use evidence-based observation tools that result in qualitative data. As they co-construct meaning from the data, leaders and teachers can make decisions about changing practice. Termed street data (Safir & Dugan, 2021) or pragmatic evidence (Cobb et al., 2018)—these data can improve instructional practices. The school leader's role—which transfers to peer observation practices—is to collect and analyze data, share the evidence with teachers, facilitate useful conversations about teaching and learning (Chapter 6), and use schoolwide evidence to inform professional learning activities (Chapter 7). As leaders and teachers grow as practitioner-researchers, they learn how to translate the data observation and analysis practices to other schoolwide concerns.

In creating the tools for the grant-funded project that we reference in this book, we addressed the critical factors of time and skills to support leaders to engage in effective teacher observations. In our analysis for this chapter, we used results from multiple participatory action research (PAR) studies in which school leaders successfully used observation tools to use classroom evidence to have conversations with teachers. Using Hale's (2008) standard of validity for the activist research goal of equity and social justice, we assert that a crucial metric of internal validity is usefulness to the participants. The participants in the leadership studies reported shifts in teacher instructional practices when school leaders analyzed daily classroom practices. Using systematic, efficient, and useful processes, teachers and leaders used iterative evidence to make incremental changes; slowly but steadily, they developed collaborative tools to accelerate collaborative change (Gomell et al., 2022; Wise & Jacobi, 2010).

As discussed in Chapter 2, nurturing relational trust is a necessary condition for school improvement and an indispensable component for achieving classroom results. By focusing on short but targeted observations and using tools to observe equitable access and content rigor, a school principal—or a district leader supporting a principal—can simultaneously be an instructional leader and a leader for equity. Using evidence-based tools and equity-driven processes, school leaders build cohesion and mediate teacher learning (Bohannon et al., 2024; Wong et al., 2020, Woo & Hendricksen 2023). Using the observations tools and the framework (Tredway et al., 2019a), teachers and leaders address the longstanding issue of equitable academic discourse (see Table 5.1; Resource 5A). The primary goals of using these practices are to increase equitable access and rigor in classrooms, base instructional decisions on learning theory, and rely on tried-and-true instructional strategies.

EQUITABLE ACCESS AND RIGOR

The grammar of schooling—the architecture and the process—has been with us since the inception of schooling; the syntax is standard—teacher's desk at the front of the room, teacher standing at the front, students in rows of desks, teacher-directed learning, and the teacher doing most of the talking. Equitable dialogue, often a stated vision, is rarely enacted—despite research evidence on the importance of access and rigor (Boykin & Noguera, 2011; Smith & Stein, 2011; Stein et al., 2015; Zwiers & Crawford, 2011). Rather, teachers typically call on raised hands, do not offer adequate think time, and use technology that supports the banking method of education, whether a blackboard, a whiteboard, an Elmo, or the ubiquitous PowerPoint (Budd, 1986; Freire, 1970; Lyman et al., 2023; Stahl, 1990). They re-enact teaching as they were taught, calcify the grammar of school, and perpetuate dynamic conservatism by changing temporarily but "going back" to the former practices (Cuban, 2012, 2023). As a profession, we fail to actualize what we know definitively about learning theory, neuroscience, and best practices.

To add to the mix, school or district leaders reinforce ineffective processes in adult meetings and professional learning. They tell teachers what to do but fail to

Table 5.1. Framework of Academic Discourse

ACADEMIC DISCOURSE (AD)			
	Teacher-Generated	Teacher Initiated and Facilitated	Student Generated
Academic Task: What the teacher asks of the student(s)	• **Designer:** Teacher-designed, directed, and controlled • **Cognitive Demand:** Typically low	• **Designer:** Teacher-initiated and facilitated • **Cognitive Demand:** Medium to high, teacher-facilitated	• **Designer:** Teacher and student collaboratively designed and facilitated • **Cognitive Demand:** High cognitive demand
Protocols and Questioning	• **Teacher Role:** Teacher-designed questions; teacher-controlled protocols • **Underlying focus:** Often compliance and behavior-driven; concerned with pacing and fidelity • **Primary interaction relationship:** Teacher-to-student; often pseudo-discourse • **Calling on strategies:** Typically raised hands; limited use of strategies for equitable access • **Level of questions:** Often recall and the application questioning levels with few questions at higher cognitive levels	• **Teacher Role:** Teacher-initiated, including encouraging student-to-student dialogue • **Underlying focus:** Student understanding and teacher use of student experiences • **Primary interaction relationship:** Teacher-to-student, with teacher encouragement of student-to-student and small groups • **Calling-on strategies:** Designed for equitable access of all students • **Level of questions:** Attention to higher cognitive level questions, including synthesis and creativity	• **Teacher Role:** Coaching students as facilitators; warm demander and strong student relationships • **Underlying focus:** Encouraging more student-facilitated groups • **Primary interaction relationship:** Student-to-student • **Calling on strategies:** Primarily student-generated questions and student-to-student interaction • **Level of questions:** Higher level questions that elicit creative responses and authentic problem solving

<table>
<tr>
<td>Dialogue</td>
<td>• Teacher role in questioning: All questions by teacher; posed for short responses; teacher often looking for right answers
• Teacher-to-student dialogue: Typically one-way dialogue and with a subset of students
• Student responses: Inaudible and short; often repeated by teacher or ignored if “wrong answer”; teacher often repeats student responses</td>
<td>• Teacher role in questioning: Most questions generated by teacher; questions range: recall to analysis
• Teacher-to-student dialogue: Focusing on extensions
» Teacher asking for elaboration and clarification
» Teacher requesting support for ideas
» Student paraphrasing encouraged
» Student questions encouraged
• Student responses: Equitable access for student responses; complex thinking and interactions in teacher–student interchanges; multiple student ideas or solutions considered; paraphrasing of student responses encouraged</td>
<td>• Teacher role in questioning: Collaboratively generated
• Teacher-to-student dialogue: Primarily coaching; focusing on probing questions for deeper learning
• Student responses: Student-to-student dialogue, often initiated by students; student-driven conversations; built on and challenging ideas of other students; ideas supported with evidence, often co-generated</td>
</tr>
</table>

effectively engage them in learning. Despite pockets of success, we have been unsuccessful at changing the instructional narrative to address effective and equitable learning—dialogue, rehearsal, co-construction of knowledge, and opportunities for metacognition (Hammond, 2015; National Academy, 2018; Vygotsky, 1978). We do know what to do, but we must be brave and consistent in our doing to respond to the long unanswered question about the black box of teaching and learning (Bryk et al., 2010; Cuban, 2013).

Learning Theory and Dialogic Learning

From Dewey (1938) to Bruner (1960) to Piaget (1968) to Vygotsky (1978) to Resnick et al. (2015) to Hammond (2015), we know how people learn (National

Academy, 2018). Yet we also know that being culturally responsive to learners—to their authentic ways of being in learning spaces and exhibiting cultural discourse patterns—is not only necessary but vital to learning (Emdin, 2021). However, instead of supporting instruction that values what we know about learning theory—particularly the importance of student experience, dialogue, and cultural ways of knowing and doing—we stick to the long-engrained teaching routines that privilege fast-paced, teacher-dominated classroom instruction. In addition, leaders push teachers to implement the proscribed curriculum with fidelity while the basics of effective learning are absent from classrooms. Dialogue is largely teacher to student, with the teacher using poorly framed questions, offering no think time for cognitive processing, and repeatedly calling on students who raise their hands. When teachers engage students in alternative forms of questioning and response patterns and use multiple forms of dialogue as foundational pedagogy, "students perceive stronger increases in their autonomy support, competence support and cognitive engagement when teachers changed their discourse practice" (Böheim et al., 2021, p. 1). To interrupt the most common form of discourse in classrooms—hand raising—teachers must be ultra-intentional because this particular grammar of schooling is deeply entrenched.

The value of dialogic learning is grounded in learning theory, social justice beliefs and practices (Freire, 1970), and motivational theory (Bandura, 1977; Brophy, 2004; Weiner, 1986). We know that students learn best through dialogue. Therefore, changing the questioning forms and levels can increase democratic participation in classrooms.

INSTRUCTIONAL ANTIDOTES: TRIED-AND-TRUE PRACTICES

No one solution or remedy can fix school challenges or outcomes. Still, for over 60 years, we have known how to observe classrooms effectively. Using these observation processes, we can better attend to equitable access and cognitive rigor. Effective classroom dialogue includes teacher questioning, think time (originally termed wait time), and student dialogue, including supporting students to ask questions (Lyman et al., 2023). Since the 1950s, Bloom's taxonomy of cognitive levels of questions has guided teacher education and teacher practice. However, over and over, teachers consistently ask low-level recall, basic comprehension, or application questions instead of planning and asking analysis or synthesis questions. Or teachers resort to nonquestions like, "Who knows the answer to . . . ?" or fill-in-the-blank questions that often begin as teacher statements and turn into questions: "The cause of the War of 1812 is what?"

To design the evidence-based observations tools, we conducted 30 classrooms observations and found insufficient think time in 90 percent of the classrooms. The basics of learning theory had been discarded—no think time leads to inadequate student responses. Recall questions with no cognitive demand result in student boredom. Lyman introduced think-pair-share (TPS) in the 1970s as an effective way to promote student thinking and responses. However, TPS—reduced to "turn and talk"—generally results in students left to their own devices to turn (perhaps) and talk (about what, they often do not know).

If students are to fully engage in the dialogue processes, including how to ask questions, they need to be explicitly taught discourse structures, and we need to honor the cultural discourse structures they bring to the classroom (Emdin, 2021). Using ThinkTrix (Lyman, 1987; Lyman et al., 2023) offers a different opportunity for student dialogue because students create questions and respond to each other. Initially developed as a response to the vague cognition levels of Bloom's taxonomy, ThinkTrix (a thinking matrix) is based on specific thinking actions: recall, similarity, difference, cause and effect, example to idea, idea to example, and evaluation. In a 7th-grade humanities class using TPS and ThinkTrix (TT), students showed an average increase in response time of 49 seconds (196%) and 100 words (147%) for each question. In Purser's (2019) study, students increased their ability to connect the text to deeper meaning from 1 to 14 attempts 3 months later, and 19 of 20 students reported that the TT question stems helped them understand on a more advanced level. Shifting teachers' instructional practices requires a school leader who can support productive data-rich observations, conversations, and professional learning so that teachers gain confidence in being and becoming teachers who value student thinking and know how to enact dialogical experiences for students.

USEFUL OBSERVATION PROCESSES

Just as we know how to effectively teach, we know what constitutes effective data-driven observational practices (Acheson & Gall, 1980; Gall & Acheson, 2013; Cogan, 1972; Glanz & Sullivan, 2000; Glanz & Zepeda, 2016; Glickman, 2002; Glickman et al., 2017; Goldhammer et al., 1993; Saphier, 1993; Sullivan & Glanz, 2013; Zepeda, 2007, 2016). Engaging in supervisory practices has a long history in the school improvement literature; starting in the 1990s, school districts recommended walkthroughs as useful ways to provide teachers feedback, and since 2009, instructional rounds have been an effective process for gathering aggregate evidence across the whole school. City et al. (2009) were quite clear about describing classroom practices, not analyzing or judging then too hastily. Yet evidence confirms teachers experienced these practices as inspections. While they may be useful to the school leader in understanding what needs changing across an entire school, instructional rounds rarely contribute to changing individual teaching practices. In a 4-year study of 150 teachers, Valli and Buese (2007) found increased teacher anxiety when a district instituted walkthroughs, and the processes are unproductive with teachers or changing classroom practices (Grissom et al., 2013). Melvin (2017) found that the use of IR, imposed by the district, did not reduce apprehensions. As teachers attempted to agree on the next level of work (an IR recommendation), they had different needs and interests in their individual classrooms, which could not be addressed by a group decision. Rather, we support a type of walkthrough tool with adequate evidence for individual teachers to make changes and have conversations in small groups about their efforts. However, what must precede its use is cultivating teachers' trust and input.

To have productive conversations with teachers about effective practice, observers need observation techniques that focus on nonjudgmental data to promote equity in individual classrooms. School leaders use selective verbatim scripting for short observations (Step 1). They use equity-based codes to analyze classroom data (Step 2). Rather than providing feedback by leaving notes after a walkthrough or dominating the post-observation conversation, leaders use evidence to guide dialogue, which is a catalyst for teacher conversations and decisions (Step 3). This three-step process of 10–15 minutes for each step addresses time concerns (see Table 5.2). Thus, school leaders who supervise with a social justice lens uphold the shared beliefs of a community, engage in critical inquiry with teachers, and continue to develop a culturally responsive lens for observing classrooms (Jacobs & Casciola, 2016).

Tools for Coding Equity-Driven Observations

School leaders and teachers as peer observers—using a set of equity-based tools for calling-on, question form, and question level—conduct brief (10–15 minutes) but useful observations. For each tool, observers use identified codes and add codes or names of practices (see Tables 5.3 and 5.4). They can use the same type of tool to adapt the tool to other topics (Tredway et al., 2019b). The codes for calling on, used in combination with using seating charts, address equitable access—who talks and responds and how often. Question form is critical for signaling student attention, the first step of information processing (Driscoll, 1994). Or, school leaders and teachers focus on question level, which signals cognitive rigor. The tools seem deceptively simply, but using them, the observers become practitioner-researchers because the tools provide specific evidence for instructional conversations.

Some codes (names of practice) represent positive examples of effective calling-on and increase equitable access (e.g., revoicing or TPS); other codes or practices are negative examples of student engagement (e.g., blurting out). For example, raising hands, the most common calling-on process, is the least effective classroom calling-on practice for equitable access; many students are "boxed out" of classroom dialogue if they are not quick to raise their hands. On the other hand, think-pair-share, used effectively with think time and pairing, is the gold star of classroom discourse and offers opportunities for every student responses (ESR) (Lyman et al., 2023). Coupled

Table 5.2. Three-Step Process for Observations

Process Steps	Activity
1. Observation	Observe classroom using selective verbatim and perhaps classroom seating chart.
2. Data Analysis	Use codes from tools to code data, design opening question based on the evidence, and share evidence with observee.
3. Post Observation Conversation	Use the *Effective Conversation Guide* process to engage in a short, data-driven conversation in which the teacher (observee) decides next steps.

Table 5.3. Calling-on Codes [Tool 5B]

CODE	Full CODE NAME	Explanation
R	Raising hand	Teacher calls on a student who raises a hand.
CC	Cold Call	Teacher cold calls on a student who did not volunteer and had little time to prepare.
WC	Warm Call	Teacher calls on a student who did not volunteer and has time to think and prepare.
CCD	Cold Call Discipline	Teacher cold calls on a student for discipline.
B-A	Blurt-out: Accept	Teacher accepts a response blurted out by a student(s).
B-I	Blurt-out: Ignore	Teacher ignores a student who blurts out an answer.
C&R	Call and Response	Teacher intentionally prompts students to answer together in unison to a known question.
ES	Equity Strategy	Teacher uses an equity strategy (e.g., choosing a name randomly) to determine which student to call on.
TR	Teacher Repeats	Teacher repeats student response verbatim.
TRV	Teacher ReVoices	Teacher revoices—uses a student response to paraphrase and perhaps ask other questions.
TPS	Think-Pair-Share	Teacher asks students to think for appropriate think time, pair, and then share.

Table 5.4. Question Form Codes [Tool 5C]

Question Form Code	Question Form Explanation
Y/N ?	Yes/no questions
QW or NQW	Question word (question starts with question word) No question word (question does not start with question word)
FIB ?	Fill-in-the-blank question
SNA	Student name after question
SNB	Student name before question
TT	Thinking time for type of question
NTT	No think time used

with effective teacher responses—not repeating student responses verbatim because that practice discourages students from listening to classmates—but revoicing, the teacher paraphrases student responses to ask probing questions.

The question form and question level [Tool 5D] are similar to the calling-on tool. In both cases, observers can note think time (TT) or no think time (NTT). Adequate cognitive processing time to ensure student learning is critical and perhaps the most common missing element from classrooms. The key factors in question form are using a question word to start a sentence and placing the student name at the end of the question after think time.

In Table 5.5, we summarize the results of 12 participatory action and activist research projects in which school leaders over time (1.5 school years) worked with a small group of teachers, co-practitioner-researchers (CPR), to shift classroom dialogue. The 12 school leaders worked with teachers ($n=55$) and conducted observations ($n=218$) and post-observation conversations ($n=157$) to reimagine use of evidence to make instructional decisions. The principal and the teachers as co-practitioner-researchers used daily data available in classrooms to shift teaching practices. In addition, they hosted 32 workshops with all teachers in their schools to pass on what they learned and interest other teachers in the processes as the teachers became ambassadors of becoming participatory researchers and change agents (all 77 EdD dissertation authors and titles are in Appendix A).

In a study of how teachers increased think time in classrooms, more students responded when given 10 seconds to think about an analysis level question (Geathers, 2023); in three studies of classrooms with a high ELL demographic, 1–2 minutes or thinking plus writing increased student responses (Abdolcader, 2023; Kasner, 2023; Lau-Yee, 2023). Teachers who use sufficient wait or think time support the learning of all students. Not only do individual students have more opportunity to respond, but the use of think time increases the number of students engaged in dialogue, signaling learning as a collaborative enterprise.

Using the question level tool [Tool 5D], leaders used familiar terms from frameworks related to cognitive levels of questions—Bloom's taxonomy, the revised taxonomy, or Webb's Depth of Knowledge—to code cognitive levels of questions (Anderson et al., 2001; Bloom, 1956; Francis, 2021). As school leaders became proficient with the tools, they combined the question level tool with the question form codes for a complete picture of questioning practices. As teachers became more confident, they realized that planning questions as a part of their lesson plans meant they asked more rigorous questions. As the teachers supported students to feel comfortable with think time and used equitable calling-on tools, more students responded with longer and more thoughtful responses.

The power of multiple studies with similar results indicates the importance of observations for collecting useful evidence to support the next step of the process—conversations with teachers. In some cases, leaders collaborated with teachers to customize or co-design an observation tool; Kasner (2023) and Lau-Yee (2023) used names of practice (codes) from the calling-on tool and from a nonverbal tool to craft a tool for observing joyful learning in classrooms with high numbers of Chinese ELL students. Teachers in the James (2023) study developed a tool for observing inquiry in high school classrooms. Customizing the tool for local use is a critical step not only in maintaining teacher autonomy in the process to maintain comfortableness, but also to "meet teachers where they are and support them in their development of culturally responsive teaching" (p. 37).

Table 5.5. Results of 12 Participatory Action and Activist Research Projects

Focus of Practice	CPR Members/ Mtgs	Obs.	POC	PD for Staff	Findings
Rigor and cognitive demand of teacher questions (HS) (Britt, 2023)	4/12	24	11	2	1. A well-facilitated community of practice supported teacher agency for effective collaboration and transfer to classroom practice. 2. Evidence-based observations coupled with observation conversations provide teachers with data to make necessary changes to their instructional practices.
Rigor and cognitive demand (MS) (Dupree, 2023)	5/5	12	5	2	1. Warm demanding learning conditions that foster their development as adult learners. 2. Teachers transfer their learning to practice when they have opportunities for peer dialogue and input on observations processes.
Inquiry teaching and learning (HS) (James, 2023)	5/8	3	3	2	1. Teachers who experienced inquiry in professional learning shifted their thinking about inquiry-based teaching by experiencing inquiry as learners. 2. Shifting teacher thinking led to implementing inquiry-based teaching practices.
Culturally responsive practices for math classes (K–5) (Geathers, 2023)	5/9	12	9	3	1. Teachers' lived experiences, perceptions, and knowledge influence their current instructional practices. 2. Principal and teacher collaboration supports incremental changes in instructional practices.

Focus of Practice	CPR Members/ Mtgs	Obs.	POC	PD for Staff	Findings
Culturally responsive practices for math classes (K–5); Ahmad (2023)	5/14	15	12	3	1. Teachers change their academic discourse routines to foster equitable access. 2. Observations and post-observation conversations facilitated by the school leader supported teachers to shift to culturally responsive practices.
Play-based learning in math (K–3) (Randhawa, 2023)	3/8	18	18		1. With intentional planning and reflection, teachers improve their instructional practices while building their capacity to integrate play-based learning. 2. By integrating instructional practices that involve peer engagement, teachers shift their practices from whole-class instruction to facilitating learning activities and observing students' play-based learning.
Culturally responsive practices for ELLs (FA/3–5) (Abdolcader, 2023)	4/14	40	34	4	1. Relational trust contributes to collaborative decisions about instructional practices. 2. Teachers play a crucial role in academic conversations. 3. Teachers use ELL-specific pedagogical tools to increase access and rigor.
Joyful learning for Chinese ELLS (K–5) (Lau-Yee, 2023)	3/10	24	17	4	1. Teachers need to engage in a set of experiences and practices that promote a sense of belonging and joyful learning so that teachers transfer learning to student learning experiences. 2. As teachers build a common definition of joyful learning, they implement CLRP strategies that fostered student access, rigor, and student independence.

Table 5.5. (*Continued*)

Focus of Practice	CPR Members/ Mtgs	Obs.	POC	PD for Staff	Findings
Joyful learning for Chinese ELLS (K–5) (Kasner, 2023)	5/8	28	6	7	1. Teachers who cultivate intentional relationships with students support a safe and joyful learning environment for students. 2. Teachers who plan and implement lessons with specific CLRP strategies support equitable access, academic rigor, and agency for ELL students.
Productive struggle for African American students (3–5) (Edwards, 2023)	5/13	18	18	1	1. Teachers focus on warm demanding to foster the necessary conditions for culturally responsive classrooms. 2. Although teachers know the attributes of productive struggle, teachers are hesitant to demand and do not easily encourage productive struggle.
Defining and implementing culturally responsive practices (MS) (Moon, 2023)	5/17	12	12	2	1. Participants demonstrate high empathy but inconsistently high expectations. 2. When a teacher is a warm demander, cognitively demanding academic discourse is much more likely to occur.
Supporting novice teachers to develop equitable practices (K–5) (Lassiter, 2023)	6/8	12	12		1. A communal learning space that includes learning through conversations influences conditions for teacher learning. 2. If we involve teachers in learning through intentional acts of knowing, their beliefs evolve about students.
TOTAL	55/126	218	157	32	

These leaders started their EdD work in a microcredential experience to learn about tools for effective evidence-based observations and conversations; then they applied to complete the graduate work in an EdD program. The themes from the research projects and studies offer direction for school change:

1. Go slow to go fast; leader patience for teacher readiness is critical.
2. Observation data provides specific usable evidence that teachers can make decisions and shift their individual teaching practices.
3. Teacher experience precedes teacher change, which we discuss more completely in Chapter 7.

As Mette and colleagues (2024) assert, "the goal is not to maintain comfortableness, but to meet teachers where they are and support them in their development of culturally responsive teaching" (p. 37). If leaders with teachers have co-constructed a holding space for adult learning—a gracious space for leading and learning, all of the school-based adults are more willing to learn in public, admit concerns, engage in conversations with each other, and feel supported to make mistakes and learn from them as they take on more equitable and rigorous practices.

Leader Patience and Teacher Readiness

We once made a video using mayonnaise-making as a metaphor for incremental change. The ingredients are simple—egg, lemon juice, dry mustard, salt, and oil. However, trying to make mayonnaise too quickly means the ingredients "break" and, like the Humpty Dumpty nursery rhyme, cannot be put back together again. The incremental process of teacher observations and the post-observation conversations (see Chapter 6) result in a slow-drip process into which key ingredients can be added—including cultivating peer observations and using data from observations to guide professional learning (Gawande, 2017). The school leader facilitates the emulsification process—a slow and steady blend of ingredients with the right timing. In mayonnaise making, once the ingredients cohere, dribbling in oil at a somewhat faster pace is possible. The same is true for teacher change; as they trust the processes and the people using them, they are more willing to be vulnerable and learn in public. Leaders need to be attentive and patient as they assess teacher readiness and adapt observations to differentiate for teachers—the same practices we expect of teachers in classrooms as they work with students.

James (2023) and Britt (2023) reported some discomfort and impatience on the pace of teacher change. However, James realized that "teachers need to see their teaching and learning *in situ*—they need to examine their classroom practices with guidance from the instructional leader to develop a professional vision of what they could and should do" (p. 159). She confirmed that "the process of working together was beneficial; teachers enjoyed learning from one another, and co-learning accelerated the process for all, even when their learning rates were different and even when success in classrooms was not immediate" (p. 162). One teacher took longer than others to take on inquiry teaching, but, with support, he expressed his appreciation for the leader's support until he could be more vulnerable and change his practices. The principal developed the ability to put aside her impatience and gradually guide, observe, confer, and slowly suggest possible choices that led the teacher to shift.

Using the observation tools, the school leader's response is factual, not judgmental or vague. By focusing on specific evidence, teachers can the decide on the changes they can and should make. As a result, teachers picked up the pace and shared their processes with other teachers in the school in Community Learning Exchanges. In several instances, they organized CLEs for the entire staff to share what they were learning. For example, in organizing a CLE on defining productive struggle, the principal with the teachers facilitated the entire staff to develop a common understanding of the term and the processes (Edwards, 2023). The principal coded the data from those conversations and presented the data to the staff so that they could develop a common language; as the teachers worked through how to enact productive struggle in classrooms, she used their language in coding other observational data. In another example, teachers volunteered their time to prepare and facilitate the back-to-school professional learning on academic discourse (Britt, 2023). Because they had benefited from the evidence from observations, they wanted to share what they had learned with staff.

Observation Data: Specific Usable Evidence

If we had a dollar for every school leader who said they were never taught how to do observations in this way and every teacher who said they never had a school leader who paid attention in this way, we would be rich. Several principals reported that they had never learned to do observations this way and the process completely changed their leadership practices (Tredway et al., 2021). Every teacher in the 12 studies found the evidence from the observations useful to their shifts in practice. The rich data responds to Hale's (2008) validity standard—usefulness to participants. The teachers and school leaders reported that observing classrooms with the tools gives them a clearer and more useful way to engage with each other and use daily pragmatic evidence available in every school.

For example, Lau-Yee (2023) had been trying to shift teachers from a sole focus on academic success to the social-emotional and sense of belonging that Chinese ELL students reported as low at her academically high-performing school. The use of observation tools provided tangible evidence of classroom practices and sharing the data with teachers. Along with CLE protocols that teachers experienced and transferred to classroom use with students, a set of practices emerged that teachers used to increase student processing time. When the Chinese ELL students used a think-write-pair-share process with up to 15 seconds of think time for questions and 1–2 minutes for writing, the result was more equitable participation. Teachers reported that their emphasis on joyful learning increased student participation and reduced anxiety about not having the right answers. The changed pacing became standard classroom practices. And, as we know from other inclusive practices, all students benefit.

Common tools—those that teachers collaboratively select and those that teachers adapt or co-design—provide a focus of sensemaking in teacher conversations and act as social and knowledge mediators (Wise & Jacobi, 2010; Wong et al., 2020; Woo & Henrickson, 2023). Tools empower users to organize and monitor mental processes such as attention, problem solving, planning, and intentional learning (Orland-Barak & Maskit, 2017). Common tools offer language for conversations, and the result is greater consciousness—in this case, greater consciousness and intentionality of teaching practices (Vygotsky, 1978).

As Norris (2022) suggests, tools support sensemaking and sensegiving; as teachers interact and analyze individual and aggregate classroom evidence, they decide on the professional learning they need to be more confident about shifting their practices. Tools provide a concrete way of developing common instructional language, which in turn prompts conversations and strengthens coherence in a school setting. Principals and teachers selected or adapted the tools to develop common language for discussing and analyzing data to make decisions about changing their practices. As a result, teachers became more conscious of access and rigor inequities in classrooms and remedied those inequities with more intentional choices.

Teacher Experience Precedes Teacher Change

Most studies had a similar finding—teachers need to have concrete and relevant experiences that precede their ability to engage in changing classroom practice. To accomplish teacher learning, principals reported that:

- Teachers need learning experiences and pedagogical processes in their learning that they are expected to use in the classroom.
- Teachers need a safe place—a holding space—to engage in what would otherwise be uncomfortable conversations about their hesitations, misgivings, and mistakes in classroom experimentation.

In the case of James's (2023) goal of more high school classrooms using inquiry instructional practices, she organized CPR meetings to mirror lesson plans for inquiry. Responding to the common issues of think time, several principals designed professional learning to include specific attention to review the key elements and variations of think-pair-share. Ahmad (2023) facilitated discussions on question level; as teachers discussed cognitive rigor and how that particularly applied to African American students, she organized professional learning on question level and rigor for the CPR group and the staff.

A CPR member statement (Britt, 2023) summarizes how a teacher felt about the process of being in the group and his learning process:

> I think with liberation comes the freedom to fail, which I felt we didn't have at first, but I appreciated that part of the process. It was awkward to have pointed out that only the white students are talking in my class and then only white males—it was a very gut punch for me. . . . I couldn't defend myself, but when I was designing the things for kids . . . the number one thing I said was everyone has to talk—and how do I get them to do that. So they made podcasts—every kid has a presentation. It [observation data]

has affected my reflection. There is a real sense of missed opportunity when I think about the day—I should have phrased the question this way or asked this question; [this process] has 100% changed how I reflect on my practice—I have a voice.

CONCLUSION

New learning requires a safe space for making mistakes and discussion—a central tenet of liberatory design discussed in Chapter 4. Teachers need time to experiment, learn, talk to others, and try again—precisely the process students often need. Teachers need school leaders and colleagues who assess adult zones of proximal development and design experiences—often with the teachers—to scaffold their learning so they can fully engage as co-learners. School leaders must model precisely what we want in classrooms in every adult learning experience. They must be ready to experience hesitation and perhaps discomfort as they design and implement new processes, use new tools, analyze evidence, and customize the tools and processes for the school community. In Rogers's (2003) diffusion of innovation theory, change must be within eyesight of what teachers already do—their adult zone of proximal development. The leader must be adept at assessing teacher readiness and capacity for shifting practice. In a circular learning environment, we collectively make and give sense and use daily and accessible qualitative evidence to become researchers of our work and enactors of our espoused visions of equitable and culturally responsive classrooms.

Resources and Tools for Chapter 5

https://www.tcpress.com/filebin/PDFs/9780807786147_supp.pdf
(See page 7 for a QR code linking to this URL.)

5A. Project I^4 Framework for Equitable and Rigorous Student Learning
5B. Observation Tool: Calling On
5C. Observation Tool: Question Form
5D. Observation Tool: Question Level

Additional sources

- **Bloom Taxonomy Original and Revised:** https://www.wbtsystems.com/learning-hub/blogs/blooms-taxonomy
- **Webb's Depth of Knowledge (DOK):** https://static.pdesas.org/content/documents/m1-slide_19_dok_wheel_slide.pdf
- **ThinkTrix:** https://www.kaganonline.com/catalog/look_whats_inside/TTT_rationale.php
- **Contact authors for additional types of observation tools.**

CHAPTER 6

Effective Conversations, Not Feedback

> Educators must shift their paradigms about what is measured, quantified, analyzed, and reflected on. . . . This means measuring things we know matter in public schools, using assets-based approaches to instruction, and then acting on the data meaningfully to make instruction more equitable and accessible.
>
> (Mette et al., 2024, p. 34)

Classrooms provide a ready source of daily data that is useful for individual teachers in shifting their instructional practices. In discussing observations, we previewed the importance of post-observation conversations, the focus of this chapter. To be clear, the typical post-observation meeting between a school leader and teacher—or, for that matter, between a district supervisor and school leader—lacks the potency for what leaders or teachers need to change practices. The interactions typically revolve around perception or judgment without sufficient evidence to support suggestions and include direct and sometimes judgmental feedback from observers.

Data too often come to leaders and teachers as "indigestible, dehumanized information" (Sharatt & Fullan, 2022, p. 2). Instead, teachers and leaders need to see specific data about their students so that they better serve students individually and collectively; as leaders discuss the evidence generated from classroom data with teachers, the teachers can make decisions about what to change. That starts with usable data from observations in which individual teachers can analyze the difference between their intentions and the actual ways they are or are not contributing to equitable student learning. These data become evidence or information that is the grist of the leader's conversation with the teacher rather than feedback from the observer.

Feedback, in general, is one person's response to another about the person's performance; ostensibly useful for improving performance, the feedback often connotes judgment. Despite best attempts, feedback is hierarchical, and the observer—usually the school or district leader—tells the teacher or leader what was observed (usually in summary form) and makes suggestions (perhaps too many) about what to do differently. Typically, the observer does most of the talking and the observee listens. We have a different idea about how the interaction should proceed, based on the belief that the teacher (or a leader observed by a supervisor) can and should make decisions about what and how to change, albeit with guidance from the observer (school or district leader, instructional coach, or peer). The change may not happen as quickly as the observer might wish, but the adult's readiness or zone of proximal development is the critical variable in the conversation (Orland-Barak & Maskit, 2017). Adults sometimes make changes when directed but return to prior practices unless they are supported to embed the practices in their instructional rituals and routines systematically. Schön (1973) named this phenomenon dynamic conservatism—change with regression because "institutions are characterized by a tendency to fight to remain the same" (p. 30); consequently, the teacher-directed, inequitable classroom endures (Cuban, 2023).

Two teacher responses affirm the usefulness of selective verbatim and coded observation tools. A teacher commented, "It is 20 minutes of good information, a true snapshot of what happened. . . . it is not evaluative, nothing to hurt you . . . based on the observation data, now I think, let's let them struggle, give them time to think, and help each other so that is what I am trying to do more of now." Another teacher confirmed, "Selective verbatim is so much better, you are probably thinking you are equitable and that everyone talks . . . but you really aren't" (Britt, 2023, p. 155). In discussing the process, we use "observer/coach" and "observee/coachee" to clarify the persons involved. The observer/coach could be a district supervisor, principal, administrator, instructional coach, or peer teacher. While most examples are principals observing teachers, the process is applicable to other relationships.

Coded data are particularly useful to observers and observees in the post-observation conversation (POC). In describing the process, we stress the importance of an opening question and the role of the observer as coach for supporting equity and capacity building. We assume the necessary conditions for change discussed in Chapter 2 are in place.

The observer offers an extra set of eyes and ears—in other words, SuperVision; the observer records precisely what happened and what was said (selective verbatim) and offers the data analysis (discussed in Chapter 5) to the observee. Then, the observer and the observee have an effective conversation using the data as information to make decisions about what to change. The precarious trajectory from the data to actual shifts in teacher (or leader) practice is fraught with possible missteps if the observer offers directives about what to change. To navigate from the observation to decisions about change efforts, three critical processes are necessary. After the observation (Step 1), analyze and develop an opening question and share the data with the observee as a starting point for the post-observation conversation (POC). In the coaching conversation (Step 3), use specific data and coaching strategies.

Using these processes constitutes activist research for changing school-based teaching practices as the school leader (observer) and teacher (observee) assume authority over daily qualitative evidence to collaboratively decide what to change. Because collaborative research of this nature requires a high degree of trust and intimacy, relational trust is a necessary condition (hunter et al., 2013), but so is effective evidence. To be activist researchers means that all efforts are directed at listening carefully to each other to enact change. Such efforts are often messy and imperfect, but small-scale efforts—characterized by localized, face-to-face intimacy and personal interactions—are the meat and potatoes of this CLE axiom: *The people closest to the work are best situated to discover answers to local concerns.*

These efforts of leading and learning together lead to incremental and sustainable change by attending to justice-centered coaching in which the observer and the observee are collaborators in the conversation (Wetzel et al., 2023).

SHIFTING TO POST-OBSERVATION CONVERSATIONS

Two Community Learning Exchange axioms address the importance of conversation as a mental model for replacing feedback: (1) *Learning and leadership are dynamic social processes*, and (2) *conversations are critical and central pedagogical processes*. The importance of dialogical learning is replete in Freire's (1970) guidance about how to decrease the banking method of instruction in classrooms (or professional learning) and deeply engage in dialogical reflection to promote shifts in action—the crux of *praxis*. In facilitating critical dialogue between the observer and the observee, *critical* means vital or essential.

In addition, the conversation reflects the tenets of activist research processes in which a group collaborates to engage in change efforts. While the observer may have individual POCs with each teacher, a small group of individuals can share evidence at meetings and learn in public with each other. Thus, participants co-create "safe conditions for open and self-critical discussion about their individual and collective practices" (Kemmis et al., 2014, p. 33). They have voluntary networks of communication among participants, respond to deficits that arise in hierarchical interactions, offer opportunities for public discourse, foster inclusion and intersectionality, and use ordinary and common language. Wetzel et al. (2023) urge observers to develop a shared language and stance with observees. As a result, they together generate communicative power that may indirectly affect the organizational systems. As they establish the criteria for communicative spaces and action, those practices for adult conversations transfer to collective dialogue as well as influence individual instructional practices.

Because time is always limited, short observations (10–15 min.) with data analysis using specific codes (10–15 min.) and a short post-observation conversation (10–15 min.) seem possible within the schedules of leaders, coaches, or peers. Eventually, teachers gain proficiency in the same qualitative research processes and become peer observers as they learn the processes for observation, coding, and coaching conversations (Figure 6.1). The school leader starts the process and gradually includes instructional coaches and teachers as peer observers when they are comfortable with the knowledge, skills, and dispositions they need to conduct evidence-based observations and facilitate effective conversations using coaching processes.

To activate and sustain liberatory, justice-centered, and culturally responsive processes that focus on equity access, cognitive rigor, and usefulness to participants, we developed tools that support equity-centered processes, a constructive-developmental approach (Drago-Severson et al., 2023), and coaching lenses and approaches (Wetzel et al., 2023; Woulfin et al., 2023). The tools provide data on how students engage in

Figure 6.1. From Individual Observations to Collective Change

Chapter 5		Chapter 6	Chapter 7
Observation (Data Collection)	Data Analysis (Codes from tool) Develop Opening Question	**Post-Observation Conversation(s) & Teacher Decision(s)**	Professional Learning Content & Pedagogy

equitable, rigorous, and emancipatory discourse, and the POC offers an experience in which the observee and the observer engage in sensemaking and sensegiving (Norris, 2022).

As a collaborative conversation about changing curricular content and instructional practices, critical colleagues collaborate for liberation—liberation from hierarchical supervision and liberation from professional learning not pertinent to the local needs (Mette et al., 2024). The principles of justice-centered coaching are useful as participants "disrupt the expert-novice divides" to engage in expertise that includes leader, teacher, and perhaps students and families, and as they center their work in "communities working for change" (Wetzel, 2023, pp. 13–14). In addition, coaching is a professional learning process that straddles the individual's thinking, organizational level improvement, and systems-level component of change (Woulfin et al., 2023). However, beliefs do not turn into a steady push forward toward enduring change unless the observer has a set of practices that support effective coaching and result in actual shifts in classroom practice.

EFFECTIVE CONVERSATION GUIDE

To shift from feedback to more authentic and useful conversations, the *Effective Conversation Guide* includes propositions and processes that we used with 216 school leaders who engaged in a federally funded project to increase their capacity to observe and have conversations about math instruction in K–12 schools (Tredway et al., 2019c; [Tool 6A]). Currently, we use the guide in microcredentials that we offer for districts and schools that want a more systematic way to improve instructional practices. We developed a set of elements for the POC process (see Table 6.1).

Several crucial components predict a successful POC process—providing evidence, deciding on a coaching stance, developing an opening question, and proficiency in coaching practices to guide the conversation and particularly the teacher's decision about what to change. The process is transferable to the relationship between a district supervisor as observer/coach and the principal as observee/coachee—especially when they conduct co-observations together.

Table 6.1. Post-Observation Conversation (POC)

After conducting an evidence-based observation,

- **Analyze and use the analysis of data** to guide the conversation; depending on the situation, **share data with teacher** before the conversation.
- Decide on an **approach/coaching stance** based on the observee's capacity and readiness and a location for post-observation conversation.
- Prepare an **opening question** based on the evidence—analysis of the data.
- Ask **coaching questions** (acknowledging, paraphrasing, clarifying, shifting, restating); summarize throughout the conversation as you move through the evidence and conversation.
- **Summarize next steps** that teacher has chosen and set date for another observation.

Coaching Stance

A general nonhierarchical stance to coaching is preferable, but school leaders as observers/coaches are aware of the varying levels of knowledge, skill, and dispositions of individual teachers and may need to choose a different stance (Mette et al., 2024). Glickman (2002) identified four stances that apply to a range of teachers: direct control, direct informational, collaborative, and nondirective. Bloom et al. (2005) name direct informational as instructional and collaborative as facilitative—moving toward transformative; they used a Mobius strip to help readers visualize how coaching is a fluid process in which the coach alternates among stances, depending on coachee responses. While the coachee needs to be a co-learner in the process, the coach's role is to use facilitative dialogue to support the observee/coachee's learning. How that happens varies. The goal is that the observee is self-actualizing and decides what to change because the observer/coach facilitates the analysis, realizations, and choices. We adapted the Bloom et al. (2005) blended coaching model (Figure 6.2), and the fluidity of the model in which the coach as the facilitator has the capacity to respond in different ways based on the responses of the coachee.

Deciding on a stance is important to the coach; by naming and practicing coaching stances, the coach can best support coachee thinking about improving practice. The process we discuss is for the large numbers of teachers, from novice to experienced, who are open to improving their practices but not for teachers who are experiencing great difficulty in their teaching. Depending on the coach's assessment, cognitive coaching that disrupts the novice–expert divide is preferable (Wetzel et al., 2023), but the observer has to be sure that the teacher is knowledgeable about possible shifts to make. If the teacher does not yet have the knowledge or skill, the coach shifts to using the direct informational stance during the coaching conversation. However, the coachee should engage in a dialogue and thinking process that is the essence of Freire's praxis—deep reflection about equity issues in order to decide on next actions.

We urge two common stances, which the coach (school leader or peer) may use to engage with the coachee, depending on the responses of the coachee (Glickman, 2002).

Figure 6.2. Adapted Mobius Strip of Effective Coaching

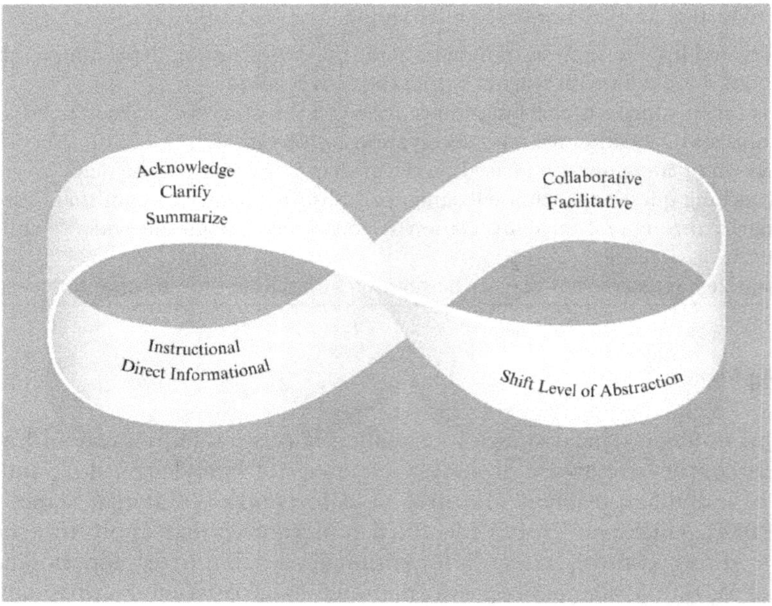

- **Direct-informational** is for a coachee who needs more information to make decisions about improvement choices; the knowledge base may not include what the coachee needs to know to make improvements. Typically, a novice teacher or a veteran who needs current thinking about best practices benefits from this coaching stance. If the conversation requires that the coach provide specific instructional direction, ask permission to be instructional—*Is it all right if I provide instructional options?*
- **Collaborative** is for a coachee who are knowledgeable about practice and for whom the evidence is supportive. The two-way conversation emphasizes teacher talk. The coach's responsibility is to ask coaching questions that elicit teacher talk and teacher decisions. The collaborative approach includes attention to nonverbal behaviors like nodding, smiling, and looking at the teacher.

The coaching process goal is co-developing a critical consciousness about practices to ensure that beliefs and knowledge about effective instructional practices match teacher actions. In dialogue as professionals and co-participants, they must confirm a shared perspective about equitable access and cognitive rigor. The coach achieves this by creating a holding space for conversation, developing thoughtful opening questions, using facilitative coaching practices, and guiding the coachee to make decisions related to the data and the coachee's readiness level (see open access videos of effective conversations identified at end of chapter).

Holding Space

Holding space for a conversation requires attention to the coachee's readiness and facilitating the physical and emotional space necessary for a productive conversation. Holding space means listening to understand and witness, modeling vulnerability and risk-taking, and, above all, making the coachee feel known and competent as well as asking useful questions. As Drago-Severson (2012) reminds us—professionals need to be confident as self-authoring knowers who can fully participate in transforming their practices. Coaches may have good intentions when offering advice, but "what really matters is how participants receive—or experience—the learning opportunity and the processes and practices that create it" (p. 49). Thus, adult learners need the same sense of feeling confident and competent that teachers hope to transmit to students.

Opening Question

The school leader's most common opening question—and the question that should be avoided—is, "How do you think the lesson went?" The question is nonspecific and requires the coachee to make judgments about performance and ineffective in promoting dialogue. Rather, the facilitator (usually observer) needs to design a question based on the data. Equally important is welcoming the observee and setting the tone for a productive conversation. The opening question is a question related to the data. Only a question based on evidence leads to a productive dialogue. If the coach does not have sufficient time to develop a specific question, use this: *What is most interesting to you in the observation data?* To see the 24 elements of productive conversations, refer to [Resource 6B].

Based on responses, the coach uses paraphrasing skills to guide the conversation. The coach affirms ideas or possibilities and summarizes to guide the teacher to a decision. Some possible opening question formats based on the collaborative and direct informational stances may be helpful (Bloom et al., 2005; Glickman, 2002; Mette et al., 2024). The goal is to have the coachee take responsibility for the data and decisions (see Table 6.2).

Facilitative Coaching Practices

After the opening question, the coach engages by listening carefully to responses, using the responses of the coachee to form follow-up questions, and shifting from listening to responding to listening with curiosity (Machado, 2021). The coach ensures dialogue by (1) paraphrasing and asking probing questions to encourage deeper thinking about data and equitable instructional practices (Table 6.3), (2) collaboratively arriving at the teacher's decision about what to change or improve, and (3) scheduling the next observation—preferably within 2 weeks (Tredway, 2006). In our experience, biweekly observations and POCs over 2 to 3 months best support coachees in experimenting, making incremental progress, and making changes that become part of their teaching repertoires. Without this regularity for supporting

Table 6.2. Post-Observation Coaching Stances and Potential Question Stems

Collaborative (Glickman) Facilitative (Bloom) Teacher who is knowledgeable about practice and for whom the evidence is supportive for their decisions about what to change.	The purpose: Coachee talking about practice. • *I observed that ______ occurred. Can we talk about that or does something else in the data stand out as important to talk about?* • *The data indicate that ______. Do they correspond to your perception of ______?* • *What was happening when ______?* • *I'm curious about this part of the observation (state factual evidence). What were you thinking about when you ______?* • *I noticed these two things about student responses: ______ and ______. What do their response indicate about their learning?* • *I noticed that you spent time with ______ and ______. I am wondering about that choice—was it purposeful or did it just happen?*
Directive Informational (Glickman) When choosing an instructional approach, get permission (Bloom). Useful for novice teachers, who often do not have a way to think through the options or veteran teachers who need particular attention.	The purpose: Coachee may need to support to make decisions about practice. • *"I observed ______. I would like to give you some options based on the evidence for that might be helpful. Is that all right?"* • *Three students on the left back and two students on right rear were talking or off task the entire period. What might you try? If no or limited response: These are three options I can think of to try: (1) ______ (2)______ (3) ______. Would any of those be helpful to you?* • *I observed that you primarily used hand-raising to call on students. You asked ______ questions; typically in those questions you did not use think time, and you called on ______ students. We agreed to in our professional learning was to use equity sticks. In this particular lesson, when could you have used those?* • *What are some other ways you know to call on students so we have more equitable access to the classroom discourse?*

transfer, the coachee easily drifts back to prior practices even when they have seen advances in student dialogue and learning. As we have discussed, dynamic conservatism easily "sets in."

Useful coaching strategies include summarizing, reframing, and paraphrasing strategically. The coach periodically summarizes to clarify and keep the conversation on track. The coach undoubtedly has some ideas about what is most important—the tricky part is not imposing a decision. Because the focus is equitable access and improved cognitive rigor, the coach guides the dialogue by reframing responses and asking questions. Besides summarizing, two strategic paraphrasing actions help—acknowledging and clarifying to ensure understanding and shifting

Table 6.3. Types of Paraphrasing and Question Stems Useful for Coaching

Acknowledging and Clarifying	Summarizing and Organizing	Shifting Level of Abstraction
By restating the essence of a statement, the coach paraphrases in order to identify and calibrate content and emotions.	By summarizing and organizing, the coach paraphrases the responses to reshape thinking and separate jumbled issues.	By shifting the level of abstraction "up," the coach illuminates other ideas and supports thinking at a deeper level. When shifting "down," the coach supports more precision.
Coaching Question Stems		
• So, you're feeling ______. • You seem to notice that ______. • In other words, you are saying that ____. • Hmm, you're suggesting that ______.	• There seem to be two issues here: ______ and ______. • On the one hand, it seems you are saying that ______. On the other hand, there might be ______ to think about. • For you then, several themes are emerging: ______, ______, and ______. • It seems you are considering this sequence or hierarchy: ______.	So, a(n) ______ for you might be ______. *Shifting up* *Shifting down* *Example to idea* *Idea to example* category example belief nonexample assumption strategy goal choice intention action option

levels of abstraction or thinking to support the teacher to think more deeply or to be specific about a concrete example.

Once the facilitator becomes adept at the process, the POC is typically 10–15 minutes. As the observer engages in several short observations and POCs with the observee, both have ample opportunity to track progress. In addition, the coach can use the aggregated information from several teachers to structure professional learning sessions for and with teachers, which we discuss in the next chapter. Teachers can share observations and plan together or make decisions about readings or activities that would bolster their knowledge and skills.

RESULTS OF ENGAGING IN EFFECTIVE POST-OBSERVATION CONVERSATIONS

We have worked with multiple participants to implement supervision practices. A total of 28 persons completed their EdD in a federally funded project; most ($n=23$) worked intensively with a few teachers ($n=3$–6) to improve practices (12 were featured in Chapter 5), and five school or district leaders worked with other principals, assistant principals, or district coaches to conduct observations and facilitate effective conversations. They managed the time factor that had previously inhibited their instructional supervision work by using the processes—observation, coding and planning an opening question, and the post-observation conversation. By chunking the process in short segments of 10–15 minutes, observers can complete the process, complete multiple observations with individual teachers, and iteratively support teachers in continuous improvement (Yurkofsky et al., 2020).

Through careful attention to coachee readiness, teachers made progress in implementing new instructional routines. More importantly, they recognized the value of evidence and conversations with principals and their fellow co-practitioner-researchers (CPR). To a person, they reported that they had never experienced evidence-based observations that resulted in useful conversations or a professional learning environment in small groups that benefited their progress.

In another example, over the course of three cohorts of a federally funded grant in which we developed these tools, school leaders ($n = 216$) learned how to conduct observations and facilitate POCs. They engaged in monthly meetings with small groups of three to five teachers, a total of 887 teachers participated in school-based, equity-centered networked improvement communities (EC-NICs) and conducted observations and post-observation conferences using the observation tools and effective conversation guide. Concurrently, school leaders participated in school leader EC-NICs facilitated by leadership coaches and attended online WebExchanges using Community Learning Exchange processes, which they transferred to their school-based meetings. Even in the year the pandemic started (2019) when teachers moved to virtual classrooms, 74 school leaders persisted in facilitating meetings and conducting observations and conversations. Thirteen leadership coaches held 150 team meetings and 814 individual coach meetings with the 74 leaders. At the school sites, school leaders facilitated 252 meetings with school-based EC-NICs ($n = 217$ teachers) and conducted 969 observations and 618 post-observation conversations.

Based on our learning from the federally funded project, we designed microcredentials—context-based professional learning experiences—for districts (Simon et al., 2021). In NYC District 2, school leaders participated in two 8-week microcredentials devoted to using the observation tools and practicing POCs. Participants used the observation processes and protocols to work with a small group of teachers to address teacher shifts in practice, particularly focusing on culturally and linguistically responsive pedagogy in classrooms. In addition to an opening and closing synchronous session, coaches met with the school leaders three times during the 8-week sequence, and they had partner check-ins with colleagues in the intervening weeks.

Of course, principals and assistant principals with large staffs, particularly in high schools, need to engage department chairs or instructional coaches in the processes. Eventually, given the right conditions for professional learning support (see Chapter 7), teachers can use these tools and practices for peer observations and conversations. At the outset, school leader modeling of the process is key—even if the leader works with only a small group of interested teachers who then become ambassadors of the work to the larger staff. As Mette et al. (2024) say, "By encouraging teachers to collect and reflect on their data, collected by peers and self-collected, schools that are engaged in culturally responsive teaching are creating infinite action research projects that will lead to more equitable outcomes *based on the needs of individualized communities*" (p. 35, italics in original). To achieve this goal, school leader(s) acting as observers and coaches must take sufficient time to learn and lead the process and encourage groups of teachers to be peer observers and engage in peer dialogue about their instructional practices.

ANALYSIS OF POST-OBSERVATION CONVERSATIONS

Some principals analyzed POCs using the same process of selective verbatim notes and naming the POC practices using the 24 criteria [Resource 6B]. Britt (2023) analyzed post-observations and determined that "evidence-based observations coupled with post-observation conversations provide teachers with data to make necessary changes to their instructional practices" (p. 137). She provided teachers with data in advance of the conversations. In her data analysis, conversations were pivotal to teachers increasing equitable access and cognitive rigor in the classroom. A teacher commented on equitable access and rigor:

> I would let Jane answer my questions and I would think that every student in the class had it, but in reality, I was letting one student speak for the class. Now, I am intentional about how I call on students and how I ask students to respond during the class period.
>
> I want to make sure my questions are there [at the higher cognitive level]. I can easily drop the questions to recall, I did it with my seniors this morning, I felt myself going down on question level to get them talking. . . . I don't want any student feeling like I am dumbing it down for them. (Britt, 2023, p. 159)

Teachers in the CPR group had individual conversations and shared their conversations in meetings. One teacher reported: "The coaching conversations were comfortable, not evaluative, informative/reflective, and an opportunity to see growth" (Britt, 2023, p. 160).

In her participatory action research study, Abdolcader (2023) conducted 40 classroom observations and facilitated 34 post-observation conversations. One important realization for the teachers was adequate think time for English language learners. While teachers knew that think time is an essential component of effective classroom discourse to promote deeper learning (Lyman et al., 2023), they sometimes ignored using what they knew because of the demands of pacing guides or instructional routines that had become habitual. One teacher reported, "I forget to think about the time essential for them to make connections" (p. 103). To practice think time and accustom students to the think time, one teacher used a timer and explained that she was more intentional about giving students ample think time after her consideration of a previous POC and discussions in the CPR group. Another teacher explained that she gave the students "time to think in their head. . . . Then they have time to process. I give them a chance" (p. 103). She had previously not given students much think time, but after discussions and readings during the PLC meetings as well as iterative post-observation conversations, the teacher incorporated this technique of time to think in her teaching practice.

In two studies on supporting Chinese ELL students (Kasner, 2023; Lau-Yee, 2023), based on POCs and group discussions, teachers relearned the value of think time. Teachers decided that inserting writing in think-writing-pair-share (TWPS) was important (Lau-Yee, 2023). When ELL students had 2 minutes to write responses to a well-developed question before the pair and share, the students had deeper responses and were more confident of their language abilities to express themselves.

In another set of POCs, Edwards (2023) employed a direct-information approach to support teachers to practice being warm demanders with African American students (Bondy & Ross, 2008; Delpit, 2012; Ware, 2006). The teachers had strong personal relationships with students and created safe spaces for learners, but teachers needed help in balancing the dual roles of building relationships and holding students to high expectations. While teachers created safe spaces for student learning, they struggled with knowing how to push students to new levels of learning and had difficulty fully implementing the role of warm demander. The principal, an African American woman of many years of experience, engaged the school staff in defining and understanding productive struggle. In the POCs after 18 observations, she modeled being a warm demander with teachers, and they role-played possible scenarios they could use with students. Speaking to the importance of teachers having experiences in what we want them to do, she said,

> I have discovered that if real teacher change is going to happen, I must model being a warm demander and push teachers. As I reflected I realized I needed to be a warm teacher demander. If teachers are to become effective warm demanders, I must push them to the same high standards they need to hold for their students. (Edwards, 2023, p. 161)

As always, school leaders need to assess the situation and make good choices about the level of readiness in the teachers and the level of support (e.g., information, modeling) that they need in order to shift teacher practices. In this school, teachers believed high expectations of students were important, but to get beyond their hesitancies, they needed modeling.

Post-observation conversations matter. They matter to the school leader as coach, who has a deeper understanding of the issues teachers are facing in implementing particular practices. They matter to teachers who need nonjudgmental support from the school leader and colleagues in making changes. The slow drip of early conversations leads to increased teacher agency and accountability for making specific classroom changes to promote equity and rigor. As they gain confidence, their ability to change accelerates. The school leader as an instructional leader can support teachers to make decisions and incorporate new practices in their instructional routines.

Scaling this work within a school is an important and doable task for school leaders. However, how can practices transfer to the district? The same process, with some adjustments, is useful for secondary school leaders and their administrative teams and district supervisors of principals who often co-observe in classrooms or conduct instructional rounds in their schools. Two studies included secondary principals working with administrative teams to support the cohesive use of observation tools and post-observation conferences (Mudd, 2023; Scott, 2023). In two other district-level studies, supervisors conducted classroom observations with the principal to understand the patterns of assets and challenges across a school (Tang, 2023; Triplett, 2019).

In tandem, the one-two punch of evidence-based observations and post-observation conversations sheds light on what needs to improve (evidence from observations) and how changes can be tested (pedagogical conversations). The tools and processes provide safe, data-informed processes for educators to improve their teaching craft and to do so with a socially just, equitable focus.

Resources and Tools for Chapter 6

https://www.tcpress.com/filebin/PDFs/9780807786147_supp.pdf
(See page 7 for a QR code linking to this URL.)

6A. Effective Conversation Guide

6B. Elements (Codes) of Effective Conversations

Other Resources

- **Effective Conversation Video 1:** https://vimeo.com/367293711
- **Effective Conversation Video 2:** https://vimeo.com/399231504

CHAPTER 7

Authentic and Meaningful Professional Learning

> There's a world of difference between insisting on someone's doing something and establishing an atmosphere in which that person can grow into wanting to do it.
>
> —Mr. Rogers

> Localized teacher learning supported and facilitated by expert teacher leaders creates scale and buy-in that is far greater than any other professional learning model.
>
> —Joshua Barrett

Throughout the book, we have stated that leaders and teachers must take charge of their professional learning—the form (content, facilitation, and pace) and function (socially just, equitable practices). As we have stressed, leaders need to set up the necessary conditions for learning and observe and guide others—often teachers—to decide what to change. In other words, a leader's role is first to establish an atmosphere in which adult learners choose what and how to change. A leader guides by understanding the growing edge for each person and supporting them to shift practices toward greater equity and rigor (Drago-Severson et al., 2023). Then, others—often teacher leaders—serve as anchors and ambassadors for their colleagues.

However, quite the opposite picture represents the educational reform landscape. In the 30+ years since the advent of the standards movement, districts often dictate how schools use professional learning time to implement proscribed curricula. At this moment, North Carolina (along with other states) has mistakenly tasked every district with using teacher professional learning time in districts and schools with LTRS phonics training, a poor substitute for what we know about effective reading instruction (Pearson et al., 2023). Too frequently, professional development facilitators use the modern and ubiquitous form of the banking method—a PowerPoint slide deck—to tell leaders and teachers what to do and how to do it without the necessary experiences or dialogue that are critical for learning. Despite best intentions, principals are often caught in a middle manager role, buffering and brokering with district supervisors to do the right thing in schools (Grubb & Tredway, 2010; Militello et al., 2009). Nonetheless, principals are uniquely situated to be bridges and buffers as they support adult learning differently. No ideal conditions are present for starting this work; leaders always operate in imperfect circumstances with multiple assets and challenges that confound change efforts. We do know, as you know, that the current state of professional learning is largely unsuccessful in changing leader and teacher practices and most definitely student outcomes. Thus, we offer an antidote, but not a surefire remedy.

Adult learning mirrors the developmental process of incremental learning principles—what Drago-Severson et al. (2023) term constructivist developmental processes. If we expect to counteract dynamic conservatism—change happening for a moment and then morphing back to old routines (Cuban, 2012; DiMaggio & Powell, 1991; Schön, 1973)—we need to approach professional learning differently. While teachers may respond for a short period of time to requests or demands to change, they rarely change their routines permanently unless they co-construct, experiment, make mistakes, and have conversations about practice shifts (Rosa & Toncelli, 2022).

Traditional professional development privileges direct instruction—"I do, we do, you do." As a result, the participants do not co-construct meaning or decide how to experiment or adapt. However, successful transfer to practice must consider a complex set dispositions, knowledge, and skills. As Dewey (1938) reminds us: "As an individual passes from one situation to another . . . what he has learned in one situation becomes an instrument for understanding and dealing effectively with the situations which follow" (p. 44). Learners who proceed on this premise may take more time initially but can accelerate change once they have sufficiently considered and experimented with their best course of action.

Transfer for teachers means adapting new learning to classroom practice by viewing the classroom as a crucible for experimentation. However, for new instructional routines to become part of teachers' repertoires, we need to model those processes in adult learning sessions. This learning process is not linear or top-down; we do not transmit knowledge and skill and then expect teachers to take up a Nike form of action—"just do it." Adult learners need experiences and conversations in which they take ownership and imagine how best to implement changes to witness if the new practice is " better than the idea it supersedes" (Rogers, 2003, p. 15). Too often, however, change is viewed as a "hurry up and do" process, which Rosa and Toncelli (2022) call drive-by learning, and Fullan (1993) calls "ready, fire, aim!" Educators know that "if an innovation is imposed upon [people], without the chance to assimilate it to their experience, to argue it out, to adapt it to their own interpretation . . . they will do best to fend it off" (Marris, 1974, p. 157). Teachers should generate ideas and adaptations as a part of implementation cycles of inquiry in which educators try new things and examine how changes impact the learners. As a result, we respond to these questions:

- How do leaders and teachers become researchers of their work and regularly use the available data to shift their practices (Safir & Dugan, 2021)?
- How can a constructivist-developmental approach to adult learning grounded in culturally responsive practices and justice-centered coaching

respond to the emotional nature of change that adults experience (Drago-Severson et al., 2023; Wetzel et al., 2023; Woulfin et al., 2023)?
- How do the school and district leadership teams assess the aggregate needs of the teacher workforce and co-construct professional learning based on teacher needs (NIET, 2018)?
- How do leaders and teachers avoid the pitfalls of isomorphism—the dynamic conservatism of returning to prior practices (DiMaggio & Powell, 1991)?

In this chapter, we discuss how the processes of evidence-based observations, conversations, and coaching transfer to a small group of teachers and then to the school organization. Our goal is to create an authentic learning organization in which adults promote learning from within (Grubb & Tredway, 2010). School leaders, instructional coaches, and teachers used accessible and regularly available data from classrooms to collectively improve practices. To demonstrate transfer, we use the evidence from school leaders who implemented the observation and conversation protocols and from the teachers they worked with. Finally, we discuss how organizational actors in schools and districts can work with groups to promote change—following the liberatory design principle of probes or small experiments before expanding to the larger context. We conclude with recommendations for enacting authentic professional community of practice. The processes we suggest breathe life into a critical Community Learning Exchange axiom—*the people closest to the issues are the best sources of addressing complex dilemmas of instructional practice.*

TRANSFER TO CLASSROOM PRACTICES: TEMPORARY OR PERMANENT?

First, we highlight the 12 principals from Chapter 6 who worked with 55 teacher participants over inquiry cycles to shift classroom teaching practices. Second, we discuss the evidence from conversations with 15 teachers from six schools who experienced the change processes we described in earlier chapters. Three themes represent the backbone of how teachers shifted their classroom practices.

1. Teachers need *emotional support* to make shifts. While teachers often articulate what they should do, they need support to be vulnerable enough to take risks and experiment with new instructional routines. In the process, the principal and fellow educators (leaders and teacher peers) support teacher confidence to change.
2. Effective professional learning requires safe spaces for teachers to *experience* new practices in collaboration. Modeling practices is not just common sense—modeling is a necessary professional learning component.
3. Once teachers are *confident*, they seek opportunities for collaboration and are *anchors and ambassadors* of change with other teachers.

The three attributes represent effective learning for adult learners (Drago-Severson, 2012; Knowles, 1980), experiential learning and dialogue as foundational to learning (Dewey, 1938; Hammond, 2015; Vygotsky, 1978), and the tenets of liberatory design (Anaissie et al., 2021), which stress the importance of using an equity lens to experiment with probes in small groups before implementing with an entire group or school.

Attending to Emotional Support

The emotional factor looms large when we ask adults to change—teachers and leaders (Wang, 2020). Not being certain of what to do or how to do it, teachers and leaders experience discomfort. Cross and Hong (2012) examined how teachers' internal perceptions of self and external demands interact; as a result, teachers often experience disappointment, frustration, and discouragement. However, they often cope with these emotions in isolation and do not have a space to address their feelings: "Relationships are not just emotional; they have a physical component. Relationships exist at the intersection of mind-body. They are the precursor to learning" (Hammond, 2015, p. 45). However, when teachers feel a sense of safety and belonging, they take risks to change (Drago-Severson, 2012). Since "much of our know-how is not inborn but painstakingly accrued" (Jackson, 2023, p. 8), teachers need a disposition of uncertainty—curiosity, experimentation, and discovery—if they want to acquire new knowledge and skills. And they need support—as leaders uncovered teacher anxiety about change, they provided differentiated coaching to teachers.

As leaders cultivated trust, the teachers reported that their relationships with the principals changed. Instead of evaluators of their teaching practices, they viewed school leaders as colleagues on a quest for understanding how to achieve goals. In small group meetings with teachers, principals used personal narratives to cultivate trust, and the tone of meetings changed. For example, when a principal used a personal narrative protocol in which teachers told stories about the tables in their lives, and one teacher said, "The table we need to set for each other as we prepare for this work must be a welcoming one, where people feel comfortable to speak their truth." As teachers experienced positive experiences in cultivating trust, they used similar protocols in classrooms [Tool 7A]:

> As teachers experienced a growing sense of belonging in our small community, they engaged in learning, tried new things, and collaborated in ways that they would not have attempted in other settings due to lack of trust or fear of being judged. One teacher said, "I'm more flexible with my teaching methods . . . I haven't explored more because of the risks of messing up. I've been better at accepting the risk and trying out new ways to engage students. (Lau-Yee, 2023, p. 140)

Teachers and students viewed the principal as a part of the class instead of a supervisory visitor. They reported a new bond with the principal and other teachers in the group and wished that more meetings and learning in the school were similar to what they experienced. One teacher expressed, "The more they know about me, the more I open up and they open up." They began to view the observation process as helpful and nonjudgmental, not a perfunctory practice of preparing a special lesson for an observation. In turn, the principal's visibility in the classes and less anxious teachers led to reduced student anxiety. One middle school principal instituted "small talks." During passing periods or in the lunchroom, he informally inquired about their families and discussed aspects of teaching. The conversations provided a springboard to cultivate trust and discuss instructional practices. Intentional informal conversations were critical to maintaining momentum for change (McDuffie, 2023).

During professional learning focused on math teachers and classrooms, two elementary principals used math journey lines to determine how teachers experienced math in their education [Tool 2F]. The levels of teachers' math anxiety—which do not fade over time—represented a potential barrier to their implementing more constructivist math practices in classrooms (Patkin & Greenstein, 2020). As Xenofontes and Andrews (2023) explain, other teachers who as students experienced math as a positive experience are confident. As a result, their pupils exhibit success, especially on abstraction and mathematical reasoning, whereas teachers who themselves experienced failure as math students do not engage in more complex math teaching and pass on anxiety to students. One teacher said, "I was never good at math, and I learned through conversations with the principals and other teachers that I might be passing my feelings on to the students, which is not something I wanted to do." The teachers were expected to teach math using constructivist methods but often had insufficient experience or knowledge about teaching math. Sharing the stories publicly decreased anxiety and increased their confidence to better support student math thinking. One teacher reported that she was more open to learning how to be a math teacher who supported students in co-constructing multiple solutions to problems and having conversations about their thinking.

Horn and Little (2010) note that in teacher discussion groups, normalizing teaching dilemmas can reassure teachers and establish solidarity, particularly if teachers focus on instructional ideas instead of more examples of the problem. As a result of the comradery and the sense that "they were in the same boat," teachers increased their vulnerability by admitting to not knowing. As a result, they took risks in classrooms that they previously were anxious about trying. A teacher said, "I continue to go to colleagues when I am stuck. As a result of this process, I am more likely to open up." When teachers exude confidence, they can make mistakes and acknowledge what they do not know; they tend to be flexible and creative and are ready to take risks (McCullouch, 2016). In fact, when teachers express uncertainty, the working memory of the brain expands, and the person is open to more possibilities (Jackson, 2023). As a result of increasing confidence through leader attention to observations and facilitating small groups of teachers to express their concerns, teachers took on new classroom practices focused on wait or think time and more equitable ways of calling on students. Developing a collegial atmosphere in a school in which the participants feel as if they can be open about their concerns has the potential to be an authentic learning space for adults as well as the children they teach.

Often, school leaders modeled the practices they expected in classrooms. In one case, teachers focused on being warm demanders of students (Edwards, 2023)—a warm demander forms relationships and can "push" the learner to new levels of cognition and skill. The principal—by having solid relationships with teachers—pushed them to shift. Initially, this caused emotional upset for teachers. One teacher said she took the principal's response personally; she cried after the post-conference and did not fully understand what to do. She was nervous about making students feel bad or think she was mean. However, as she realized that the principal was modeling what she wanted her to do, she said, "I said to myself—wait, now I understand. She was not saying I was a bad teacher; she was saying that I needed to add this to my repertoire and that it's possible because I am a good teacher." The teacher changed from a fixed to a growth mindset about her teaching and realized she had been modeling the opposite of what she wanted for students.

The teacher's anxiety represents the "growing edge" of self-authoring that Drago-Severson (2023) identifies as a growth pattern in change efforts. The teacher's main worry was what the principal thought of her. She recognized that "Kids might cry; we cried with Dina (the principal), but we pushed through and understood because we had a relationship and trusted her and she trusted us." The teacher changed her approach to students by saying, "I know you are upset that I am pushing you, but you can do this and I am here to support you"—the same disposition and language the principal used with the teacher. Supporting teachers through the emotional responses is complex, and getting inside and underneath these shifts instead of just assuming quick change is the complex work of transformational change. A teacher now in a district-level coaching position said: "It is now a routine to discuss how relationships are intertwined with academics. I share what a warm demander is with teachers I coach. I ask—can I push you on that?"

By recognizing the emotional component as central to change, we garner potential for enduring change—diminishing the possibility of teachers trying for a short time and discarding. Evidence-based observations and conversations aided principals in having meaningful conversations and teachers in transferring practices. Inside the veritable black box of teaching is the heart work—the affective domain of working with teachers. Emotional bonds of trust and conversations about complex practice issues bind teachers and leaders to each other in ways that bring life to the adage: "Every day in the classroom is a thought experiment."

Modeling Strategies

The principals facilitated professional learning meetings with small groups of teachers and/or the full teaching staff by effectively using the learning from classroom evidence to construct learning agendas. The school leaders used the protocols that they wanted to see in classrooms that also supported learning experiences for teachers. As one principal stated, personal connections translate to the classroom and affect professional interactions (Lau-Yee, 2023): "As teachers had joyful experiences in their learning in small group meetings, they expressed increased enthusiasm and willingness to try new strategies" (p. 139). When teachers experience communal learning and instructional strategies as learners, they are more likely to incorporate those practices in their classrooms, which comports with Dewey's (1938) basics of learning as experiential—a continuity of experiences that inspire reciprocal growth and interactions.

In an effort to encourage more joyful and equitable learning of emergent bilingual Chinese American learners and use culturally and linguistically responsive (CLRP) practices, the principal and staff experimented with think time (Lau-Yee, 2023). Knowing that emergent bilingual learners need more processing time, the principal expanded think-pair-share to think-write-pair-share (TWPS). The principal reflected,

> I was tempted to talk or explain during silent moments, but I learned to wait in case someone was processing. For those who were not verbal learners and could not readily absorb reading texts, we read small excerpts and rehearsed and shared our thinking after Think-WRITE-Pair-Share. The more we practiced articulating joyful learning and CLRP characteristics, the more we could articulate CLRP and what joyful learning looked and felt like in classrooms. (Lau-Yee, 2023, pp. 124–125)

The teachers shifted from turn and talk, in which students had no time to think about responses before they responded, to the crucial components of think and pair in order to share (Lyman et al., 2023). They realized that longer think time resulted in more student talk in pairs and added writing to think time (see Figure 7.1). The principal reported,

> Teachers used a variety of strategies to elicit student dialogue, collaboration, and communication . . . and provided space to write or draw. They asked higher level questions and used longer think/processing time before students shared. Teachers assigned collaboration partners and used sentence frames and roles so that students knew how to communicate. One teacher noted . . . , "I'm glad that I'm able to see other perspectives and change direction at these meetings. It helps me to remember that there are many different perspectives and emotional responses to every moment shared by a community." (Lau-Yee, 2023, p. 120)

This example offers one among many of how principals documented evidence in classrooms for teachers so that they could discuss evidence [Tool 7B]. The cyclical nature of dialogue routines resulted from conversations between the teachers and the principal. The practice situations and discussions helped teachers experience the difference as they implemented and experimented in their classrooms. TWPS was a result of the experiments and interactions.

In shifting instruction in a high school, the principal worked with four teachers over 2 years to encourage inquiry-based instructional practices by gearing their meetings to inquiry processes, including using different questioning practices. As James (2023) indicated, "Teacher practices only change once they have personally experienced and engaged in new learning using the strategies for their learning that we expect them to use in the classroom—in sum, once they have had an opportunity

Figure 7.1. Teachers Work With the Principal to Improve Instructional Practice

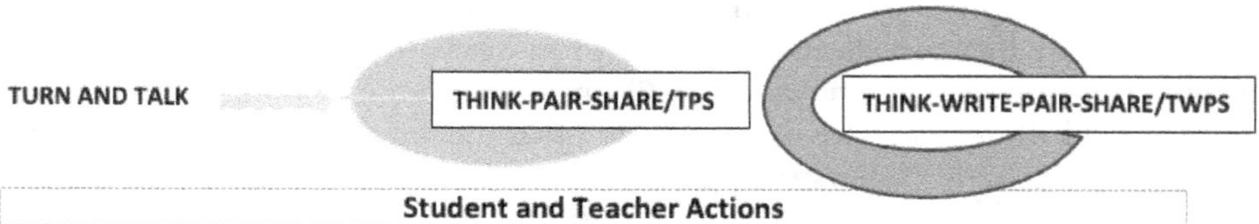

Student and Teacher Actions		
• Students turn to anyone informally (often more than one person) • No think time - turn right after teacher question • Often used by teacher to break • Teacher waits	• Students have assigned partners • Think time (5–15 seconds) • Turn to face each other intentionally • Take turns in pairs to talk • Rehearsal in pairs leads to more participation in full group • Teaches go to specific students to listen and probe; may ask them to start sharing	• Students have more time to write responses • Think time (15 sec.–2 min.) • Produces more complete thoughts • Students more relaxed and confident about participating in large group • Teachers can assess individual student learning, ask probing questions

to co-design what to do" (p. 133). As a result, the group co-developed a tool for observing inquiry-based classrooms [Tool 7C].

Britt (2023) and Ahmad (2023) identified higher-level questioning practices. As they modeled those questions in small groups and in full staff meetings, teachers realized they needed to plan questions with a higher cognitive level. Britt (2023) discussed how teachers shifted,

> After receiving two rounds of observation data, the CPR team decided on two strategies to improve rigor and discourse in the classroom. . . . Two participants discussed the need to make sure they planned questions and gave students the questions ahead of time to think about their responses, especially as the cognitive level of the question increased. A teacher stated, "Our kids can do this stuff, but I need to do more front loading and more prepping." (p. 122)

Ahmad (2023) facilitated professional development on open-ended questions. Teachers differentiated between open and closed questioning, analyzed cognitive levels of questions, and planned for questioning for an upcoming lesson. She observed that

> Teachers placed students in small groups or pairs to encourage academic discourse . . . and used protocols (e.g., round robin or roulette spinners) to determine turns for student talk. When students struggled to explain their understanding of concepts or procedures, teachers asked probing questions to scaffold their thinking as they provided clues to guide the students toward the response. Teachers learned to be comfortable with student productive struggle and give students sufficient wait/think time as they redirected or paraphrased questions to help students successfully identify how to solve problems. (p. 122)

In the evidence from multiple schools, we note a common thread—teachers need to experience strategies that promote equitable and rigorous instruction in their learning *before* they can effectively use the processes with students. As they experimented in short cycles of inquiry with CPR members, they experimented, discussed, and tweaked strategies. If we want to ensure that individual teachers transfer their professional learning to classroom practice, learning has to include experiences in the processes and strategies that support student learning.

Promoting Schoolwide Transfer: Anchors and Ambassadors

By working with a small group of teachers who become anchors and ambassadors for change, transferring the practices to the entire staff is not only possible but more probable. We caution going too fast with too many people before attending to a crucial element of the process—trial and error or a probe in the National Equity Project (NEP) liberatory design process. If we use predictable solutions, we miss the possibility of deeper change. To focus all improvement on equitable outcomes for students, teachers need to practice, make mistakes, and revise their work by using evidence to make decisions about next steps. However, these probes—small experiments with strategies we have documented throughout this chapter—require concerted effort on the part of the school leader and a small group of teachers before encouraging the entire staff to participate.

Teachers in small groups with deep experience in changing their practices are ready to be anchors and ambassadors for school change. A principal, even in a small school, cannot conduct multiple observations of every teacher; instead, the principal works with a small number of persons (three to six) and facilitates regular meetings, observes, and facilitates post-observation conversations with some teachers. When a small group is ready to share with others formally and informally, they co-facilitate learning for and with their peers.

The teachers with whom we spoke described the learning experiences as having high expectations for teachers in the same way we need high expectations for students. They viewed learning as a daily practice that motivated them to be aware of their practices and think about other ways to improve. Teacher comments included:

- "I am more aware in moments of my teaching and more intentional."
- "Observations and conversations changed how I can be demanding and expect more rather than thinking I am being strict."
- "The data made me want to try harder."
- "I feel more self-actualized as a teacher."

They were eager to engage other teachers in their school and wanted all teachers to have the opportunity to participate in small groups to nurture collaborative learning. One teacher said, "I started to think about how to talk about this on my grade level team and PLC or other teacher affinity groups." They wanted to bring what they learned to other teachers and teams.

In several instances, teacher groups co-designed Community Learning Exchanges for the staff and modeled processes and protocols they had learned and used. Four high school teachers with the principal planned a professional learning session at the start of a school year to share the observation tools and their learning about questioning. In an elementary school, the principal and teachers organized a Community Learning Exchanges on the meaning of productive struggle. By using the evidence from the group posters, all teachers developed a common understanding [Tool 7D].

In another school, teachers facilitated dialogue on instruction for English language learners by converting the district's suggested strategies into an observation tool. In two schools, the principals worked with a small group of teachers to develop an observation tool for joyful learning and share that for input from the full staff. In a middle school, the instructional support team worked with the principal to revise the schedule and provide tools for peer observers to support beginning teachers. These examples point to the possibility of teachers with leader support organizing professional learning opportunities for their peers and slowly but surely facilitating homegrown responses to school reform efforts.

In a New York City middle school, the principal and five teacher-mentors participated in a microcredential experience of two 8-week sessions. They engaged with an external coach/facilitator to use evidence-based observation and conversation tools. The five teacher-mentors provided an anchor for work across the school. With the principal, they encouraged the professional learning community structure of quads or four teachers to conduct inter-visitations using the calling-on observation tool. The principal and the teacher-mentors targeted professional learning time to work with teachers to calibrate the tools and the processes for effective conversations and encourage inter-visitations for the quads. In collecting aggregate data from 33 observations, the initial schoolwide evidence on effective calling-on strategies (see Chapter 5) indicated that teachers still prefer hand-raising and cold calling on specific students as the most common participation practices. They facilitated professional learning about think time and equitable calling on. The teacher mentors who teach half time and coach serve as anchors and ambassadors of change efforts.

We re-emphasize that adult experiences that include dialogue need to precede change efforts. These experiences should focus on attending to how adults process change emotionally, modeling effective practices, and having conversations about what and how to change practices. These considerations offer a different way forward for leading and learning from within.

REIMAGINING DISTRICT AND SCHOOL LEADERSHIP

A critical barrier to school-level professional learning is district authority. We fully understand that a district wants to build coherency for curriculum and instruction, but district policies and professional development decisions often strangle site-based agency and efficacy (Coburn, 2005; Coburn et al., 2012). Instead of responding to the complexities of a school or district, a bright idea becomes an initiative in a hot minute—the district adopts the idea and often hires outside consultants to make it happen. Typical scaling occurs too quickly and squashes the reform effort because the adult learners have no say in what happens to them. Yet, scaling could be a dynamic phenomenon *if* teams encourage active participation to explore possibilities to adapt and reinvent (Morel et al., 2019). Our processes for transfer favor adaptation and reinvention at the school level, and districts ought to better consider how to support school level adaptation (Barnett, 2023). Thus, we urge caution for district leaders—directing all principals to participate in any effort the district assistant superintendent may think is important often exacerbates the school-level improvement process. All leaders—school or district—need to consider the varied experiences of school leaders and teachers (the wisdom of people) and the individual school context (the power of place).

A district-level project points to a different possibility for leadership learning (Principal Leadership Institute, 2010). For 2 years in the elementary division of San Francisco schools, external leadership coaches worked with principals and their supervisors to co-design monthly professional learning termed equity-centered PLCs. Principals made choices about professional learning topics, and each facilitator met with a principal from the group to co-design the agenda for monthly principal meetings. Twelve groups (five to eight principals in each group) chose topics: English language learner instruction and services, walkthroughs and teacher observation, culturally relevant teaching; cross-school planning; guided reading, K–8 issues, and effects of trauma on learning. Characteristic of principal responses, one principal said, "The overall PLC process was placing more responsibility on the principals and, as such, recognized our experience and expertise." One principal reported that "getting ideas from others dealing with the same issues, getting help problem-solving helped most of all by providing me with a safe environment and peers to talk to, and that helped relieve the sense of being alone in trying to effect change." In surveying principals about usefulness of the professional learning, 90 percent of the principals reported this type of professional learning as having significant impact on their learning and leadership. Using the critical friends consultancy protocol fostered reflective leadership practices, and leaders generated concrete plans for addressing thorny issues [Tool 2J]. At the end of the school year, the principal groups shared their learning with peers and district supervisors.

By supporting adult choice for learning, respecting the collective expertise that peers could offer each other, and investing in facilitators, the district demonstrated how internal professional learning could be organized with minimal expense and maximum principal as learner satisfaction. In one example, six principals formed an affinity group of Asian American educators who served schools with high numbers of Chinese American emerging bilingual students. The facilitator conducted classroom observations with each principal, and the group used the evidence to focus on equitable dialogue in classrooms. The group read research, collected and analyzed school data, articulated the benefits of think-pair-share, and organized a professional learning on equitable classroom discourse for all teachers in the six schools.

Other contexts demonstrate how school and district leaders could and should work with schools. A school leader organized the middle school administrative team to meet monthly over the 2021–2022 school year; they collectively addressed educational equity and culturally responsive theory, frameworks, and practices (Payne, 2023). The school principal, as facilitator, found four foundational elements contributed to deepening equity leadership—adult learning spaces, rituals and routines, leadership identity development, and tools as mediators of learning. He relied on the premise of gathering as a sacred act (Parker, 2018). One participant in the group stated,

> I feel lucky to be comfortable in a room of people with the power to influence policy and practice and to work alongside people with similar visions. This has inspired me and reframed my thinking about my work and how to go about it, and I think this calmer, more patient, and more "big-picture" perspective is making me a more optimistic, hopeful, and confident leader. (Payne, 2023, p. 145)

As a result, they accelerated their learning about recognizing and attending to equity issues by engaging on a daily basis in short conversations to solve issues.

A district leader in an urban district organized four principals to breathe life into a district mandate to improve conditions for African American learners (Quadros-Meis, 2021). Rather than a technical exercise of planning goals and outcomes, the district leader cultivated a brave space for the leaders to co-develop a pedagogy of care for themselves and others and support an authentic space for vulnerability, trust, and reflection (Brown, 2018). The leaders engaged in getting to know African American families by facilitating "family wisdom circles." As a result, the district leader shifted school leader responses from transactional to transformative (see Table 7.1) and developed their knowledge, skills, and dispositions as equity leaders as they moved from being sympathetic leaders to attempting to be co-conspirators (Love, 2019).

Velasco (2021), a district leader, worked with four women district and school leaders; they cultivated an *espacio sano*, a safe and healthy space to address work-related stress as leaders of equity. They shared wellness strategies and co-generated testimonios to rely on their "brave hearts" to disrupt normative professional development spaces in schools and districts. The leaders learned to operate in a third space, a place where they co-designed their learning and established the rituals that would best support them to gain knowledge and skill. Like an equity-centered professional learning community, the school and district leaders practiced self-care as a necessary condition for maintaining resilience and focus on their values of collective strength and social justice leadership. As the *espacio sano* became a vibrant place for learning and doing, they transferred the processes to their school and district offices.

Each example exemplifies the ways that district and school leaders can shift their practices and those of other leaders. We know what works in adult learning, and we know what happens in the black box mystery space between learning new knowledge or skills and transferring practices to the professional repertoires of teachers and leaders. We just need the will to change how we act at the school and district level to do what we know.

Table 7.1. Culturally Responsive School Leaders Continuum

Sympathy	Empathy	Allyship	Solidarity	Co-conspirator
"Sympathy is feeling *for* them. Sympathy is giving advice and judgment disguised as concern." (Brown, 2018, p. 137)	"Empathy means 'to feel with.' Empathy requires the suspension of assumptions, the letting go of ego, and the release of the privilege of nonengagement." (Howard, 2016, p. 79)	"Allyship is working toward something that is mutually beneficial and supportive to all parties involved. Allies do not have to love dark people, question their privilege, decenter their voice, build meaningful relationships with folx, working in the struggle, take risks, or be in solidarity with others . . . ally-ship is performative." (Love, 2019, p. 117)	"Solidarity work may require us to give up power and/or to risk our physical safety, our jobs, our secure place in any social hierarchy, our friendships, and family relationships. Solidarity is talk *and* action. Solidarity work is often enacted by, or *in collaboration with*, marginalized people. (NYU Solidarity week website, 2020)	"The time-consuming and serious critique and reflection of one's sociocultural heritage–which includes identities related to race, ethnicity, family structure, sexuality, class, abilities, and religion—taken side by side with a critical analysis of racism, sexism, White supremacy, and Whiteness is the groundwork of coconspirators." (Love, 2019, p. 118)

Courtesy of Myra Quadros-Meis.

CONCLUSION

Based our experience, leaders and teachers can become researchers of their work and organize professional learning that is more relevant to their context if they do the following:

- Cultivate the necessary conditions for change
- Attend to participants' emotional needs as they engage in the change process
- Support adult readiness and choices
- Facilitate professional learning that models the kind of learning they seek for students in classrooms
- Set up the structures that offer adult learners as teachers and leaders time and opportunity

However, leaders must be careful about the pace—by adhering to the liberatory design principles of starting small and working with an anchor group, they can become the ambassadors for change efforts across a school or a district. The adult zone of proximal development is real, and their emotional safety in making changes coupled with modeling are critical factors in transferring learning to classroom practice. Based on what we have learned from school leaders across the country, if we shift professional learning practices for adults, then we can expect transfer—the kind of transfer that recognizes the complexity leaders and teachers face, supports experimentation, and employs real-time evidence to make decisions about next steps.

Too often professional learning is one size fits all, and strategies are implemented in schools and districts without attention to teacher readiness and developmental levels. These efforts have a short shelf life. Cuban (2023) analyzed what happens when school reform efforts fizzle. Tyack and Cuban (1997) refer to "tinkering" instead of deeply changing the grammar of schooling. Much like the framing of complicated and complex, tinkering efforts are fraught with opportunities of trying to change but quickly return to the same old ways of teaching. For that reason, we set out to learn about what happens in the in-between spaces—the mysterious interstices of school reform efforts—in which efforts have currency for a time but often fade quickly, and teachers resume former practices. We can say with confidence that learning and leading from within provides an antidote to current and largely ineffective practices.

Resources and Tools for Chapter 7

https://www.tcpress.com/filebin/PDFs/9780807786147_supp.pdf
(See page 7 for a QR code linking to this URL.)

7A. Personal Narrative: Setting the Table
7B. Observation Tool: Joyful Learning
7C. Observation Tool and Rubric: Inquiry
7D. Collecting and Analyzing Group Ideas: Productive Struggle Example

CHAPTER 8

Leading and Learning With Joy and Justice

> Joyful learning is engaging, empowering, and playful learning of meaningful content in a loving and supportive community. Through the joyful learning process, [learners are] always improving knowledge of self and the world.
>
> —Joyful Learning Network

Our lodestar is not another set of steps, a prescription, a magic elixir that guides educators to improved leadership and student outcomes. As you have seen in the book, our recommendations are not necessarily new but provide a human-centered approach in which collective leadership is a function in an organization. A metric of success is the ability to enact change with an eye and heart on joy and justice (Ginwright, 2016). Such leadership insists on collaboration with (not for) others, trusting relationships, and the power of place and wisdom of people. To begin the book, we defined the tenets of such leadership (see Figure 8.1). We illustrated our approach to leadership with stories from practice, including evidence from participatory action and activist research projects conducted in schools and districts like the places where you work and strive for change. The confluence of stories and evidence of *Leading and Learning Together* offers school and district leaders and teachers specific tools to cultivate normative leadership practices from within. The tools and practices help merge daily practice with research processes that support practitioners in taking back the rightful role of decision-makers in their contexts. School and district leaders are uniquely situated to become practitioner-researchers and facilitate these processes by engaging others to use evidence from their context to inform change. Together, as practitioner-researchers, they can transform practices in schools and districts. Equipped with engaging, inclusive pedagogies, change can be cultivated from within.

In this final chapter, we highlight leaders' reflections—school and district leaders who exemplify the leadership pivot by using pedagogies of trust and community as text. Specifically, we analyze the reflections of dissertations and microcredential experiences. For us, the reflections provide evidence about their transformations of practice. We retrospectively looked at the dilemmas, questions, and problems that have driven the leaders represented in this book. What did this type of leadership look like *after* the leaders completed the EdD or the microcredential? Did

Figure 8.1. Tenets of Leading and Learning Together

the pedagogical approaches (tools and protocols), data construction process, and Community Learning Exchanges become normative practices for leaders? How do leaders continue to authentically engage teachers, students, families, and community as assets? Themes emerged from the leadership reflections from the EdD dissertations (see Appendix B for the list of dissertations).

The book's throughline and leadership reflections based on evidence are clear. We questioned several norms in educational leadership and flipped the traditional narrative: Leadership is a collective, not a solo, act; particular kinds of data become aggregate evidence and information that are useful for change efforts; and time and professional learning can be recalibrated to enact leading and learning together. What, then, is effective leadership and learning from within? When a critical mass of educators jointly take on the work, practitioner-researchers use Community Learning Exchange processes and protocols to engage others and transform teaching and learning practices.

Leadership from within is not enacted alone. Even after a generation of critiques of the hero principal (Bush, 2020; Grubb & Flessa, 2006; Ishimaru, 2013; Sutton & Gong, 2021), "strong leadership" is too often envisioned as directive, solo work. Not surprisingly, in a context of heightened expectations placed on school leaders to address an ever-growing list of system mandates and societal problems, this emphasis on going it alone means that education systems see shortages of interested candidates to take on school leadership positions because current models of leadership are unsustainable (Bottery et al., 2018). The Grissom et al. (2021) study reasserts that the principal is of central importance for school change and improvement. Fair enough, but the principal is not the *only* one responsible; as a facilitator, the principal can join together with many others to learn and lead from within.

Traditional leadership models focusing on the principal could be more sustainable for the designated leader and the school constituents if they adopted the practices we forward. This book illustrates that *leadership from within* is facilitative, collective work rather than the work of an individual expert with an answer to every question. Schools and districts don't need superheroes; they need educators motivated by equity, driven by curiosity, and supported by protocols and trusting relationships. The strategies in this book are approaches to pulling on the same oar, meaning a leader can't be the only one moving the boat along if you want it to head in the right direction. The book provides both models and evidence of how working together from within can be accomplished.

Leadership from within cultivates a pedagogy of trust. Where does trust come from? The vision that emerges from this book is that trust is not primarily a sentiment; it's an action—developed through reciprocity and collectively doing the equity work to improve teaching and learning in classrooms. Trust is collectively developed and sustained over time when we approach equity work in particular ways. The pedagogy of trust—including processes that are inclusive and iterative—is designed to inform continuous activity, not a one-time event. The leadership pivot includes a move to authentic engagement with teachers at every meeting, observation, and professional development activity. Such leadership requires visible, often incremental efforts using protocols that invite reflection, vulnerability, risk-taking, dialogue, and, ultimately, action.

Leadership from within means concrete conversations about teaching practice not "feedback." Dozens of the school leaders we worked with dropped the "feedback" model and engaged in two-way conversations using daily evidence available in schools. "I noticed that over time, I did less talking and more listening . . . and acted as a facilitator of learning. This was a major shift in my leadership because I am used to doing the talking and fixing" (Cooper, 2023, p. 174). Another principal noted her shift from feedback to conversation because of evidence-based classroom observations:

> I learned to appreciate that the data could be used to leverage action. . . . I learned the importance of holding coaching conversations with teachers as opposed to giving them direct feedback. [This process] promoted self-reflection . . . [and] led to teachers naming their own areas for change. (Ahmad, 2023, pp. 104, 205)

Leadership from within uses time differently. Time is all too often an excuse or barrier. Sustainable change requires re-evaluating the use of time spent interacting with teachers. When mindfulness, storytelling, and self-care that guide and support teachers are baked into adult learning practices, leaders noted the differences in how participants responded. Many leaders we worked with described the impact of dynamic mindfulness for self-care on themselves and their teachers. One principal indicated that by using dynamic mindfulness, the teachers centered themselves on being fully present and preparing for the work ahead. By using personal narratives, leaders emphasized the importance of the pedagogy of trust as an iterative process. Storytelling is part and parcel of our approach; as one educational leader said, "These structures provided members with opportunities to center themselves on the work, time to learn about one another, opportunities to discuss their thinking, and time for reflection" (James, 2023, p. 169). As leaders and teachers honored and celebrated each other and their craft, they provided credence to the leadership pivot that liberates the false narrative that "there is no time." In fact, they more fully realized their goals of change through pedagogies of trust and community as text.

Leadership means dropping the either-or framing. John Dewey (1938) said, "Mankind [*sic*] likes to think in terms of extreme opposites. It is given to formulating its beliefs in terms of Either-Ors, between which it recognizes no intermediate possibilities" (p. 17). Such binary thinking (theory/practice; head/heart; equity/excellence; reflection/action) creates great divides in our field. In particular, navigating the either/or question of leadership or management has been a refrain in leadership discussions. What's so wrong about teaching and learning as management *and* leadership (Flessa, 2021)? Absolutely nothing! Instead, leaders as managers need to develop the five minds of the manager: "(1) Self—the reflective mind (2) Organizational—the analytical mind (3) Context—the worldly mind (4) Relationships—the collaborative mind and (5) Change—the action mind. If you are a manager, this is your world!" (Gosling & Mintzberg, 2003, p. 2). Leadership from within means reflecting and acting on new ways to manage schools—necessary tasks for school leaders who set up systems for achieving goals. For example, one principal built a master schedule "that staggered schedules among grade levels so that teachers could visit classrooms throughout the day to be peer coaches and observe classroom practices" (Cruthis, 2024, p. 122). Like curriculum and pedagogy inform one another, leadership and management are not binary. For school leaders, combining leadership and management requires intentional and sustained engagement, "to be an equity-centered school leader, I need to plan purposefully with solid and intentional protocols" (Mudd, 2023). Protocols are a form of management that uses time effectively for authentic engagement.

Make no mistake: Educational leaders can be dismissed more quickly for mismanagement than for inequitable student outcomes. Leadership from within means getting the management aspect of their work right. The management aspect of the leadership pivot includes planning and facilitation for existing and new routines to meet equitable outcomes; inclusive and effective alignment of efforts and goals; evidence-based decisions for policy and classroom practices; and transparent processes that center teacher and student voice and experience. This work requires that those facilitating meetings do so differently by carefully and consistently using protocols to establish a collective, equitable vision. A vision without a means to get there is a luxury that schools, leaders, and communities cannot afford. As a result, practitioner-researchers mobilize both leadership and management. Through authentic engagement and storytelling and using intentional and inclusive protocols that influence and expand collective effort and reflection, people work together for joy and justice.

Throughout the book, evidence from EdD students and microcredential participants authenticated the practices we support. However, the real test of the work is how leaders embed these practices as permanent ways of knowing, being, and doing—not change for the moment that morphs back to routines, but an authentic and intentional change in how they do the work. In conversations with teachers who worked with leaders in the EdD programs, we documented evidence of how classroom observations and evidence-based conversations reshaped their classroom teaching practices: "My principal comes all the time, so I do not have to plan something special." Another stated,

> I did not feel like I was being evaluated or judged . . . instead the conversations [based on observational evidence] helped me be more cognizant and intentional. Reflecting on the evidence informed my practice . . . I now understand what is meant by the level of student engagement.

The teachers, acting as practitioner-researchers with their principals, recognized the benefit of mindfulness practices for centering, personal narratives for sustaining trust, and evidence to shift their classroom practices. They found a different way to actively change their practices and rely on colleagues to support their inquiries into their practices.

These testimonials are reinforced with evidence from school and district leaders. Janette Hernandez (ECU EdD, 2019) facilitates CLEs with district coaches using the teacher observation and conversation tools. Marcos Garcia (ECU EdD, 2021) is facilitating Community Learning Exchanges to enlist families and community partners in supporting the district graduate profile design and implementation. Barnaby Payne (ECU EdD, 2023), a high school principal, now uses the CLE axioms in his new school as "powerful tools . . . that [demonstrate how] well-facilitated dialogic constructivism is a means to individual and collective liberation" (p. 167). He committed to continuing the work "so that I can manifest a commitment to understanding the strengths and challenges in school and district communities from the people closest to the issues and ensuring authentic collaboration toward innovative and iterative improvement" (p. 168). These are just some of the many examples of what is important—that the work leaders do in this way becomes a part of who they are as well as what they do—and they engage others to work with them as co-leaders in the process.

However, good intentions are often met with unyielding resistance. The systemsworld is a fortress built to withstand change and retain a status quo that amplifies hierarchy and dominant cultural perspectives and practices. However, by cultivating change with Community Learning Exchange axioms and processes coupled with the principles of the leadership pivot, a pedagogy of trust, and community as text, we propose a different path to the same goal—equitable learning for teachers and leaders who then transfer practices to classrooms to achieve social justice goals. We ask you to trust your lifeworlds to inform the system and your context. Rather than planning an assault on the institution, the goal is awakening the system from within. "Within" is a double entendre—within means evoking the spirit inside to examine self, and it means crossing boundaries to work from within the entrenched systems to create trust in a school or district through authentic engagement and collaboration.

Embracing new leadership practices is not easy—not easy to learn and not easy to implement. Yet we submit these practices as possible and vote for an enduring possibility—understanding and actively transforming the black box of leadership that supports learning—that is, building relational trust, ensuring the necessary conditions, and engaging in Community Learning Exchanges that prioritize empathy, adaptability, and inclusivity to foster a culture of collaboration and innovation. The authentic leadership we advocate requires a recommitment to the calling of your vocation. This is a journey with others. A leadership legacy is based on who you are and what you value but also on what you do—the processes, the normative practices that break down the political and institutional forces that bind innovation and progress—especially progress to equitable outcomes. Leading and learning together requires breathing joy and justice into our actions—the processes of imagining, planning, acting, reflecting, hoping, and reimagining again. Transforming practice simultaneously feeds the need for leading joyfully and aims at justice to improve teaching and learning for all students.

Aristotle said, "Where your talents and the world's needs cross, there lies your vocation." As educators, we chose this vocation because of the intersection of our gifts and assets and the deep hunger for education in our schools and communities. What does this intersection look like for you? What talents do you have to meet the needs of your school and community? This book is a call to use evidence-based leadership practices at this intersection. We shared our stories and those of the leaders with whom we have had the privilege to work as evidence of *leading and learning together*. We invite you to tell your story as an educational leader and set the conditions for others to share theirs. In these ways, we can bring joy and hope into our work and actualize our social justice goals. By *leading and learning together*, we cultivate the equitable change our students and communities need and deserve—from within.

Glossary

Academic (and Equitable) Rigor: A standard of excellence that teachers expect from students. To achieve rigor in classrooms, teachers create active and dialogical learning environments with appropriate support for students as they develop conceptual understanding, procedural knowledge, skills, and fluency in content areas and application to new contexts.

Access: An initial step of equitable dialogue is access. Access ensures the teacher, leader, or facilitator uses processes that guarantee and promote equitable possibilities for all participants to think, formulate ideas, and effectively engage in dialogue.

Brave Space: The conditions that adults or students need to grow and learn so they can engage in social justice conversations and actions. Participants exhibit vulnerability, examine intentions, think critically, inhabit others' perspectives, and lean into fear and discomfort.

Circular Leadership: A style of leadership that depends on reciprocity and trust for interaction and decision-making rather than hierarchical assumptions about expertise and authority. All team members are expected to contribute and collectively make decisions that affect the group.

Coaching Stance: The perspective or position a coach takes in a conversation with a coachee to support the coachee's level of readiness and experience. The perspective shifts from facilitative and collegial to instructional depending on the topic.

Community as Text: The community includes the people in schools; the school district; and organizations with a past, present, and future. Their history, experiences, hopes, and dreams offer a source of learning from multiple "texts" and a resource for deciding on appropriate actions.

Conscientização: Critical consciousness and reflection support the power of transforming the current reality. The organizational actors can work collaboratively and interrupt oppressive conditions by perceiving and acting on social, political, and economic contradictions.

Constituent: Replacing stakeholder in the educational lexicon, a participant who has a vested interest in the goal and outcome of any school or district change effort. Each person as a citizen-participant maintains reciprocity and interdependence with other organizational members.

Constructivist-Development Theory: Learners actively co-construct knowledge through learning experiences with appropriate supports and challenges that respond to individual readiness levels. Learners continue to grow and develop throughout their lives by engaging in experiences and dialogue with others who support their growth and development.

Critical Pedagogy: The teacher and student learning in dialogue with each other to counteract the prevalent banking method of education in which the student receives, sorts, and stores the teacher's deposits of information.

Dynamic Mindfulness: A body and mind process that includes mindful actions (A), breathing (B), and centering (C) to increase equitable access and learning, increase joy and justice, and center on self-care to continue the work of social justice in schools and districts.

Effective Conversation: In an effective post-observation conversation, an observer (school leader or peer) and the observee use evidence and dialogue to support teacher decisions.

Evidence-Based Practice: To inform change efforts in schools or districts, participants, as organizational actors, integrate the best available local data and evidence with research-based findings, their expertise and values, and particular circumstances to make individual, group, or community decisions.

Gracious Space: A space is gracious when the facilitators attend to the setting and spirit as an invitation to the "stranger" (person or idea) to learn in public. Participants take risks, remain vulnerable, build and sustain trust, and collectively support change efforts in a gracious space.

Journey Line: Based on Dewey's (1938) theory that "an experience arouses curiosity, strengthens initiative, and sets up desires and purposes that are sufficiently intense to carry a person over dead places in the future . . . every experience is a moving force. Its value can be judged only on the ground of what it moves toward and into" (p. 38), individuals document their experience, tell stories, and observe common patterns.

Liberatory Design: An approach to addressing equity challenges and change efforts in complex systems that meshes human-centered design with complex systems theory and equity practices. Teams use the flexible process to address equity challenges and innovate with an emancipatory systems focus. https://www.nationalequityproject.org/frameworks/liberatory-design

Lifeworld: The foundation of the social, intellectual, and other forms of human capital that contribute to cultural capital in an organization. The lifeworld—the everyday world that we share with others—should be the force that drives and humanizes the systemsworld.

Microcredential (MC): A goal-oriented learning experience that stresses iterative reflection and practice in particular knowledge and skill to achieve equitable outcomes for adult and/or student learning. The MC involves short learning experiences (4 to 8 weeks) with necessary conditions, pedagogy of trust, activities, coaching, and a capstone.

Necessary Condition: Building trust supports change efforts. We highlight necessary conditions through trust pedagogies—arts integration, dynamic mindfulness, and gracious space. These conditions facilitate trust building so that organizational actors can cultivate equitable change from within.

Pedagogy of Trust: An abstract resource that organizational actors co-create and cultivate. Facilitators use personal narratives and culturally responsive and equitable practices to cultivate trust.

Personal Narrative: A prose narrative, poem, or graphic in which organizational actors describe or tell their life stories. Based on a common prompt, they share stories and co-create humanizing systems. Storytelling is a primary source of cultivating trust and a resource for resolving conflict.

Practitioner-Researcher: Educational leaders and teachers who facilitate the collection and analysis of evidence with colleagues to inform their practice.

Self-Care: Attending to the social-emotional factors in the lives of education professionals. To undo the harm of the system's responses to children and families, self-care is the backbone of caring for others so that social justice leaders and teachers maintain resilience.

Sensegiving: The art of translating sensemaking into practice by others. Through an invitation to an inquiry process, the leader and teachers engage in iterative processes for understanding and action.

Sensemaking: The act of making sense of an environment or experience. People give meaning to their own and collective experiences.

Systemsworld: A world of instruments or procedures and policies usually experienced in schools and districts as management systems. A systemsworld emphasizes the efficiency and technical solutions to school and district issues, reinforcing a hierarchical approach to leadership and contributing to social reproduction instead of innovation.

Transfer: Applying learning (knowledge and skills) to new circumstances. Teachers and leaders view their work in classrooms, schools, or the district as places of experimentation, evidence analysis, and decisions about which actions most effectively address goals of excellence and equity. In short, leaders enact their role of practitioner-researchers with teachers, students, families, and community members.

Resources

BOOK WEBSITE

Throughout the book, we have provided resources as examples and evidence of transfer into practice. The tools and resources are identified in the text as a tool or resource, listed at the end of each chapter, and organized by chapter on the Teachers College website [https://www.tcpress.com/filebin/PDFs/9780807786147_supp.pdf].

MICROCREDENTIALS

We offer an online learning experience using many of these tools in a series of microcredentials (MCs)—personalized and flexible learning experiences based on discrete skills and competencies. Each educational leadership development microcredential (ELD-MC) is an 8-week learning experience. Each ELD-MC has three synchronous sessions with coaching and site-based practice between sessions and contains five learning components: (1) developing new knowledge of the content, (2) engaging with new tools for practice, (3) practicing in one's setting, (4) ongoing coaching meeting (1:1 and with small groups), and (5) presenting a capstone component to document and share competencies that were learned. We currently offer ELD-MCs in the following topics:

- Evidence-Based Observations for Equitable Academic Discourse
- Authentic Community Engagement
- Race and Rurality
- Trauma-Informed Schools
- De-escalating Challenging Behaviors

For more information, visit sites.ecu.edu/eld/

ECU INTERNATIONAL EDD

We derived much of the data we analyzed as evidence for this book from the graduates of the ECU EdD. The EdD was designed in 2014 based on (1) the Carnegie

Project on the Educational Doctorate principles to reclaim the EdD from the PhD (www.cpedinitiative.org), (2) an "off-model" executive MBA program design, and (3) galvanizing a practitioner-researcher approach to research that transforms practice beyond the dissertation and degree completion. All students engage in three cycles of inquiry using participatory action/activist research with an equity focus of practice. The fourth cohort of students graduates in May 2025. The complete list of graduates and dissertation titles is in Appendix B.

For more information, visit education.ecu.edu/intedd/.

ECU EdD Program Scope and Sequence

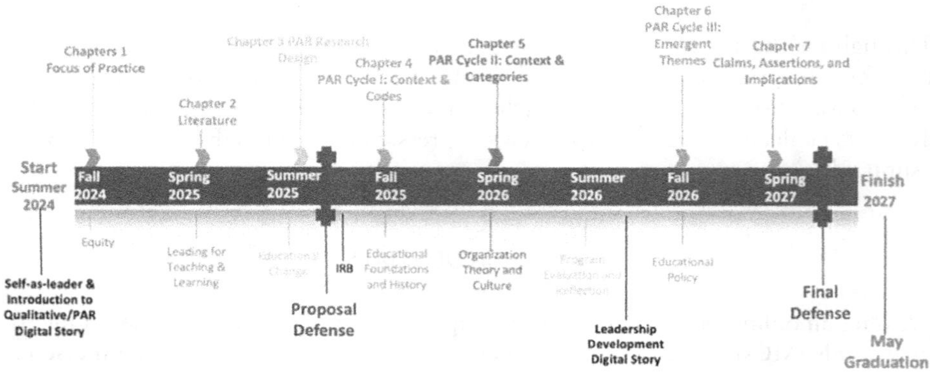

EdD Dissertations of Practitioner-Researchers

We have been honored by your work in the EdD programs. Although we have referenced some dissertations in the book, we have learned from all of you how practitioner-researchers can engage small groups to accomplish important results.

INTERNATIONAL COHORT I (2016–2019)

- **Karling Aguilera-Fort,** Reimagining principal support: A participatory action research project to engage principals in an equity-centered professional learning community
- **Esther Combs,** Authentic engagement: A rural community's journey to cross agency collaboration
- **Kristin Halligan,** Collaborative curriculum development and implementation: Inquiry-based learning as a centerpiece for school change
- **Janette Hernandez,** Going against the grain: Reimagining the role of high school principals and principal supervisor as adaptive leaders
- **Tosca Killoran,** Equity agents: Creating an innovative learning culture with foreign teachers and *lǎoshī* within an international school context
- **Prerna Paryani,** Teacher evaluation that matters: A participatory process for growth and development
- **Christie Powell,** Nimble or not? Pivoting an international school to embrace culturally and linguistically diverse practice
- **Michael Purser,** Pump up the volume: Amplifying student dialogue in 21st century ELL classrooms
- **Lori Richardson Garcia,** Utilizing Community Learning Exchanges to empower all voices and strengthen community engagement in an international middle school
- **Lihi Rosenthal,** Fits and starts: One elementary school's journey toward trauma-informed leadership
- **Ken Simon,** Inquiry: A pedagogy for personal empowerment, collaboration, and democracy
- **Mark Triplett,** Talk smart: A participatory action research project implementing academic discourse in an urban middle school

- **James Welch,** Moving from the middle: An exploration of student experiences transitioning to high school in international settings
- **Jodi Willard,** You can't give what you don't have: A community of care among special education supervisors

INTERNATIONAL COHORT II (2018–2021)

- **Mihoko Chida,** Implementing creativity in an international school: A case study of possibilities and challenges
- **Tom English,** Teacher readiness, belonging, and cultural awareness: A model for international teacher induction
- **Marcos Garcia,** Social justice warriors: Coaching teachers to develop culturally responsive pedagogy
- **Zarmina Hotaki,** Dual language learning: Using first language as a scaffold for second language acquisition and learning
- **Leila Kayed,** Reinventing how teachers and leaders co-generate equitable evaluation practices for teacher growth and development
- **Moraima Machado,** Family stories matter: Critical pedagogy of storytelling in fifth-grade classroom
- **Norah Olaly,** Developing an ecology of co-teaching: An ethnographic study of a co-teaching partnership
- **Michael Palmer,** Connecting the dots: The intersection of teacher readiness and principal actions
- **Myra Quadros-Meis,** Cultivating brave space: How networks fortify school leaders to ensure equitable outcomes for black youth
- **Alejandro Ramos,** Voices of hope: Youth of color in continuation high schools
- **Luis Rodriguez,** Beliefs and relationships matter, Critical pedagogy tenets as a foundation for changing teacher practices
- **Christina Velasco,** *Espacio sano*: How social justice educational leaders cultivate caring and sharing
- **Aaron Willette,** What's culture got to do with it? A social emotional learning program in an international school
- **Mary Yung,** Portraits of relentless progressives: Equity work in complex educational organizations

INTERNATIONAL COHORT III (2020–2023)

- **Vern Caruz,** Kapwa (shared identity): Filipino American perspectives and responses to educational leadership
- **Gretchen DePoint,** Utilizing wellbeing practices to deepen connections among international middle school leaders

- **Paul Koh,** Finding leadership 정 (belonging): A critical race ethnography of Asian American leadership
- **Gina Lappe,** They're speaking: Gender identity, agency, and belonging in an international middle school
- **Ann Ledo-Lane,** Using creative practices to foster arts integration: Supporting experiential pedagogy for teachers
- **Shannon McMahon,** Educators for gender equity: Promoting gender equity in an international elementary school
- **Kacey Molloy,** Honoring cultural diversity in an international school: How culturally responsive practices support teacher collaboration
- **Carrie Morris,** White women educational leaders: Embodying antiracism in eastern North Carolina
- **Barnaby Payne,** Experiential conditions for educational equity in action: Culturally responsive leadership development in an international school
- **Nicole Pierce,** Voices of resistance: How women antiracist educational leaders address the tensions of leading for racial equity
- **Marla Silversmith,** Reimagining student engagement in district decisions: With student voice
- **Tyler Stinchcomb,** Introducing translanguaging practices in an international elementary school: The critical role of instructional assistants
- **Wesley Tang,** Equity warriors: Building principal capacity to enact culturally responsive leadership

INTERNATIONAL COHORT IV (2022–2025)

- **Adrian deAlba,** Leading from within: How teacher leaders develop and implement a project-based model in an alternative school
- **Monica Guzman,** Improving instructional practices in literacy: Supporting the growth and development of intervention specialists
- **Alyssa Lund,** Cultivating supportive and caring IEP processes for students and families
- **Matthew Lindner,** Deep roots: Empowering teachers of elementary gifted students in inclusive classrooms
- **Arthur Sosa,** Developing teacher capacity for implementing an International Baccalaureate PYP program at an elementary school
- **Jennifer Steiner,** Cultivating beloved school communities: How school leaders learning and leading for equity
- **Lena Sweeney,** Applied liberatory design: Empowering paraprofessionals as educators
- **Suniqua Thomas,** Don't let them fall through the cracks: Using effective case management to keep our students at a comprehensive high school

PROJECT I[4] EDD GRADUATES (2020–2023)

- **Fowzigiah Abdolcader,** Using equitable pedagogy to support English language learners in academic conversations
- **Zarina Ahmad,** Black students matter: How teachers equitably engage African American students in understanding conceptual mathematics
- **Lyndsay Britt,** Creating a home: Promoting equitable academic discourse by establishing teacher agency and co-design
- **Gabriel Chilcott,** Greater than the parts: How school leaders and central office administrators build trust and coherence
- **Lori Collins,** The sweet spot of mentoring minds and building support
- **Robbin Cooper,** Language is not my hurdle: Improving equitable instructional practices for English language learners one classroom at a time
- **Krystal Cox,** Listen, reflect, act: A participatory process to support first-generation early college students using storytelling
- **Carl Cruthis,** Tacit leadership: Orchestrating teacher leadership to develop a peer coaching program for inquiry-based instructional practices
- **Leon Dupree,** Repositioning our thinking: Using culturally responsive practices to increase equitable access to rigorous instruction
- **Dina Edwards,** Cultivating equity warriors: Empowering educators to enact responsive pedagogy for African American students
- **Carin Geathers,** Getting into good trouble: Building culturally responsive teacher practices for African American student success in mathematics
- **Virginia Gilchrist Jacobs,** Seeking to belong: A PAR project striving to infuse culturally responsive pedagogy in classrooms
- **Monica Jacobson,** The bridge: How an innovative, collaborative team of principals and curriculum specialists support equitable instruction in secondary mathematics
- **Jennifer James,** Leave this place better than you found it: Facilitating inquiry-based learning experiences
- **Mimi Kasner,** Joyful learning matters: Teacher practices in amplifying joyful learning experiences for Chinese English language learners
- **John Lassiter,** The missing piece to teacher induction: A framework for adding equity-focused support to induction
- **Diane Lau-Yee,** Leap for joy: Amplifying joyful learning outcomes for Chinese ELL students
- **Norman McDuffie,** Equitable classrooms require equitable practices: How do teachers develop and implement culturally responsive teaching in support of equitable classrooms
- **Michael Moon,** Islands of innovation: Examining the nexus between culturally responsive relationships and cognitively demanding academic discourse
- **Kim Moses,** Build a village: Cultivating productive relationships with African American parents for increased family engagement

- **Kelly Anne Mudd,** Reimagining teacher induction: A framework for an asset-driven, equity-based induction process that cultivates knowledge of self, context, and professional practice
- **Timothy Mudd,** Butts, books, buses, and better instruction: How a principal can develop assistant principals into equity-centered instructional leaders by juggling tasks together
- **Johanna Parker,** Collaborative spaces for leaders: A participatory action research study to improve district and school leader collaboration
- **Amandeep Randhawa,** Play is learning: A pedagogy for building teacher capacity with integrating play in math instruction
- **Marie Roberts,** Reclaiming alienating environments: African American female principals reflect to build math identity and implement culturally responsive coaching
- **Hugh Scott,** Filling the void: Building and sustaining cohesive and consistent instructional leadership
- **Debra Windley,** We choose not to "shut up and dribble": Listening to student voices in an alternative learning school
- **Rashida Yellock,** Culturally responsive practices: Influencing teachers' disciplinary and instructional practices

General Resources for Leading and Learning Together: Cultivating School Change From Within Community Learning Exchange

CONTACT INFORMATION FOR AUTHORS

We are available to talk to you about Community Learning Exchanges and micro-credentials or other questions you may have about the resources we reference in the book. For example, we have multiple examples of personal narratives that we could not print in the book due to necessary permissions, but we can send to you via email.

Lynda Tredway: lyndatredway@gmail.com
Matt Militello: militellom14@ecu.edu

GENERAL URLS FOR INFORMATION AND OTHER RESOURCES

ECU (East Carolina University) EdD Program: https://education.ecu.edu/intedd/
ECU (East Carolina University) Microcredential: https://sites.ecu.edu/eld/
Project I^4 Tools and Resources: https://education.ecu.edu/projecti4/resources/
Institute for Educational Leadership Protocols: iel.org/protocols
Center for Ethical Leadership: https://www.ethicalleadership.org/gracious-space.html

References

The dissertations cited in the book appear at the end of the reference section and are available through East Carolina University Joyner Library.

Acheson, K. A., & Gall, M. D. (1980). *Techniques in the clinical supervision of teachers: Preservice and in-service applications.* John Wiley & Sons.

Aguilar, E. (2018). *Onward: Cultivating emotional resilience in educators.* Jossey-Bass.

Allensworth, E. M., & Hart, H. (2018). *How do principals influence student achievement?* University of Chicago Consortium on School Research.

Anaissie, T., Cary, V., Clifford, D., Malarkey, T., & Wise, S. (2021). *Liberatory design mindsets and modes to design for equity.* National Equity Project.

Anderson, G. L. (1996). The cultural politics of schools: Implications for leadership. In K. Leithwood, J. Chapman, D. Corson, P. Hallinger, & A. Hard (Eds.), *International handbook of educational leadership and administration* (Vol. 1, pp. 947–976). Kluwer Academic.

Anderson, L. W., Krathwohl, D. R., Airasian, P. W., Cruikshank, K. A., Mayer, R. E., Pintrich, P. R., Raths, J., & Wittrock, M. C. (2001). *A taxonomy for learning, teaching, and assessing: A revision of Bloom's taxonomy of educational objectives.* Longman.

Argyris, C., & Schön, D. (1974). *Theory in practice. Increasing professional effectiveness.* Jossey-Bass.

Argyris, C., & Schön, D. (1978). *Organizational learning: A theory of action perspective.* Addison Wesley.

Argyris, C., & Schön, D. A. (1996). *Organizational learning II: Theory, method and practice.* Addison Wesley.

Bailey, J. (2019, May 20). Social change happens at the speed of relationships. Strive Together. https://www.strivetogether.org/social-change-happens-at-the-speed-of-relationships/=

Bandura, A. (1977). *Social learning theory.* Prentice Hall.

Barnett, J. H. (2024). *Unleashing teacher leadership: A toolkit for ensuring effective instruction in every classroom.* ASCD with National Institute for Excellence in Teaching.

Battiste, M., & Henderson, S. (2020). Indigenous and trans-systemic knowledge systems (ᐃᐣdᐃgᐁᓈᐣ ᐠᓄᐤᐪᐁdgᐁ ᐊᐣd ᐟᕒᐊᐣᐢᐢ+ᐢᑌᒥᐨ ᐠᓄᐤᐪᐁdgᐁ ᐢ+ᐢᑌᑦᐢ). *Engaged Scholar Journal, 7*(1), i–xvi.

Benham, M. K. A., & Cooper, J. E. (Eds.). (2000). *Indigenous education models for contemporary practice: Our mothers' voices* (1st ed.). Routledge.

Benham, M. K. A., & Napier, L. A. (2002). An alternative perspective of educational leadership for change: Reflections on Native/Indigenous ways of knowing. In K. Leithwood & P. Hallinger (Eds.), *Second international handbook of educational leadership and administration* (pp. 133–165). Kluwer Academic Publishers.

Blank, M. J., Melaville, A., & Shah, B. P. (2003). *Making the difference: Research and practice in community schools*. Institute for Educational Leadership.

Blignaut, S. (2019, August 19). *7 differences between complex and complicated*. https://sonjablignaut.medium.com/7-differences-between-complex-and-complicated-fa44e0844606

Bloom, B. (1956). *Taxonomy of educational objectives: The cognitive domain*. David McKay.

Bloom, G., Castagna, C., Moir, E., & Warren, B. (2005). *Blended coaching: Skills and strategies to support leadership development*. Corwin Press.

Bohannon, A. X., Coburn, C. E. , & Spillane, J. P. (2024). Research hidden in plain sight: Theorizing latent use as a form of research use. *American Education Research Journal, 61*(3), 610–641.

Böheim, R., Schnitzler, K., Gröschner, A., Weil, A., Knogler, M., Schindler, A. -K., Alles, M., & Seidel, T. (2021). How changes in teachers' dialogic discourse practice relate to changes in students' activation, motivation and cognitive engagement. *Learning, Culture and Social Interaction, 28*, 100450.

Bondy, E., Beck, B., Curcio, R., & Schroeder, S. (2017). Dispositions for critical social justice teaching and learning. *Journal of Critical Thought and Praxis, 6*(3), 1–16.

Bondy, E., & Ross, D. E. (2008). The teacher as warm demander. *Educational Leadership, 66*(1), 54–58.

Bose, B. K., Ancin, D., Frank, J., & Malik, A. (2017). *Teaching transformative life skills to students: A comprehensive dynamic mindfulness curriculum*. W. W. Norton.

Bottery, M. (2016). *Educational leadership for a more sustainable world*. Bloomsbury Academic.

Bottery, M., Ping-Man, W., & Ngai, G. (2018). *Sustainable school leadership: Portraits of individuality*. Bloomsbury Publishing.

Boykin, A. W., & Noguera, P. (2011). *Creating the opportunity to learn: Moving from research to practice to close the achievement gap*. Association for Supervision and Curriculum Development.

Brill, F. S. (2008). *Leading and learning: Effective school leadership through reflective storytelling and inquiry*. Stenhouse.

Brophy, J. (2004). *Motivating students to learn* (2nd ed.). Routledge.

Brown, B. (2018). *Dare to lead: Brave work, tough conversations, whole hearts*. Random House.

Brown, B. (2021, December 11). The physics of vulnerability. *Daily Good*. https://www.dailygood.org/story/1973/the-physics-of-vulnerability-brene-brown/

Bruner, J. (1960). *The process of education*. Harvard University Press.

Bryk, A. S., Gomez, L. M., Grunow, A., & LeMahieu, P. G. (2015). *Learning to improve: How America's schools get better at getting better*. Harvard Education Press.

Bryk, A. S., & Schneider, B. (2002). *Relational trust: A core resource in schools*. Russell Sage.

Bryk, A. S., Sebring, P. B., Allensworth, E., Luppescu, S., & Easton, J. (2010). *Organizing schools for improvement: Lessons from Chicago*. The University of Chicago Press.

Budd, M. R. (1986). Wait time: Slowing down may be a way of speeding up! *Journal of Teacher Education, 37*(1), 43–50.

Bush, T. (2020). Turnaround leadership in education: A restatement of heroic leadership or a flawed concept. *Educational Management Administration & Leadership*, *48*(1), 3–5.

Butler, J. K., & Cantrell, R. S. (1984). A behavioral decision theory approach to modeling dyadic trust in superiors and subordinates. *Psychological Reports*, *55*(1), 19–28.

Cary, V. (2018). *Leading for equity in complex systems: Racial equity leadership network.* AERA Conference Paper.

Christensen, L. (2009). *Teaching for joy and justice: Reimagining the language arts classroom.* Rethinking Schools.

City, E. A., Elmore, R. F., Fiarman, S. E., & Teitel, L. (2009). *Instructional rounds in education: A network approach to improving teaching and learning.* Harvard Education Press.

Claiborne, S., Wilson-Hargrove, J., & Okoro, E. (2010). *Common prayer: A liturgy for ordinary radicals.* Zondervan.

Cobb, P., Jackson, K., Henrick, E., Smith, T. M., & the MIST Team. (2018). *Systems for instructional improvement: Creating coherence from the classroom to the district office.* Harvard Education Press.

Coburn, C. E. (2005). Shaping teacher sensemaking: School leaders and the enactment of reading policy. *Educational Policy, 19*(3), 476–509.

Coburn, C. E., Russell, J. L., Kaufman, J. H., & Stein, M. K. (2012). Teachers' advice networks teacher sustainability and ambitious reform. *American Journal of Education, 119*(1), 137–182.

Cogan, M. L. (1972). *Clinical supervision.* Houghton Mifflin.

Cosner, S., De Voto, C., & Rah'man, A. A. (2018). Drawing in the school context as a learning resource in school leader development: Application-oriented projects in active learning designs. *Journal of Research on Leadership Education, 13*(3), 238–255.

Cross, D. I., & Hong, J. Y. (2012). An ecological examination of teachers' emotions in the school context. *Teaching and Teacher Education, 28*(7), 957–967.

Cuban, L. (2012, August 9). *Dynamic conservatism and stability in teaching.* https://larrycuban.wordpress.com/2012/08/09/dynamic-conservatism-and-stability-in-teaching/

Cuban, L. (2013). *Inside the black box of classroom practice: Change without reform in American education.* Harvard University Press.

Cuban, L. (2023). *The enduring classroom: Teaching then and now.* University of Chicago Press.

Darling-Hammond, L., & Sykes, G. (1999). *Teaching as the learning profession: A handbook of policy and practice.* Jossey-Bass.

Dei, G. J. S., Karanja, W., & Erger, G. (2022). *Elders' cultural knowledges and the question of Black/African indigeneity in education* (*Critical Studies of Education, 16*). Springer.

Delpit, L. (2012). *"Multiplication is for white people": Raising expectations of other people's children.* The New Press.

Dewey, J. (1916). *Democracy in education.* Touchstone.

Dewey, J. (1938). *Experience & education.* Touchstone.

Diamond, A., & Ling, D. S. (2016). Conclusions about interventions, programs, and approaches for improving executive functions that appear justified and those that, despite much hype, do not. *Developmental Cognitive Neuroscience, 18,* 34–48.

DiMaggio, P. J., & Powell, W. W. (1991). The iron cage revisited: Institutional isomorphism and collective rationality in organizational fields. In W. W. Powell & P. J. DiMaggio (Eds.), *The new institutionalism in organizational analysis* (pp. 63–82). University of Chicago Press.

Drago-Severson, E. (2012). *Helping educators grow: Strategies and practices for leadership development.* Harvard Education Press.

Drago-Severson, E., Blum-DeStefano, J., & Lawrence, D. B. (2023). *Growing for justice: A leadership continuum of leadership capacities and practices*. Corwin.

Driscoll, M. P. (1994). *Psychology of learning for instruction*. Allyn and Bacon.

Duane, A., Casimir, A. E., Mims, L. C., Kaler-Jones, C., & Simmons, D. (2021). Beyond deep breathing: A new vision for equitable, culturally responsive, and trauma-informed mindfulness practice. *Middle School Journal, 52*(3), 4–14.

DuBois, W. E. B. (1903). *The souls of Black folk: Essays and sketches*. McClurg & Co.

Dweck, C. (2007). *Mindset: The new psychology of success*. Ballantine.

Emdin, C. (2021). *Ratchetdemic: Reimagining academic success*. Beacon Press.

Flessa, J. (2021). Reflection on MIE's anniversary. *Management in Education, 35*(1), 64–65.

Flessa, J. J. (2012). Principals as middle managers: School leadership during the implementation of primary class size reduction policy in Ontario. *Leadership and Policy in Schools, 11*(3), 325–343.

Foster-Fishman, P., Nowell, B., Deacon , Z., Nievar, M. A., McCann, P. (2005). Using methods that matter: The impact of reflection, dialogue, and voice. *American Journal of Community Psychology*, *26*(3–4), 275–291.

Francis, E. M. (2021). *Deconstructing depth of knowledge: A method and model for deeper teaching and learning*. Solution Tree.

Freire, P. (1970). *Pedagogy of the oppressed*. Continuum.

Fullan, M. (1993). *Change forces*. The Falmer Press.

Gall, M. D., & Acheson, K. A. (2013). *Clinical supervision and teacher development: Preservice and inservice applications*. John Wiley & Sons.

Ganz, M. (2011). Public narrative, collective action, and power. In S. Odugbemi & T. Lee (Eds.), *Accountability through public opinion: From inertia to public action* (pp. 273–289). The World Bank.

Gawande, A. (2017, January 23). Tell me where it hurts. *The New Yorker*, 36–45. http://www.newyorker.com/magazine/2017/01/23/the-heroism-of-incremental-care

Gay, G. (2000). *Culturally responsive teaching: Theory, research, and practice*. Teachers College.

Ginwright, S. (2016). *Hope and healing in urban education: How urban activists and teachers are reclaiming matters of the heart*. Routledge.

Glanz, J., & Sullivan, S. (2000). *Supervision in practice: 3 steps to improving teaching and learning*. Corwin.

Glanz, J., & Zepeda, S. (2016). *Supervision: New perspectives for theory and practice*. Rowan & Littlefield.

Glickman, C. D. (2002). *Leadership for learning: How to help teachers succeed*. Association for Supervision and Curriculum Development.

Glickman, C. D., Gordon, S. P., & Ross-Gordon, J. M. (2017). *SuperVision and instructional leadership: A developmental approach* (10th ed.). Pearson.

Goldhammer, R., Anderson, R. H., & Krajewski, R. J. (1993). *Clinical supervision: Special methods for the supervision of teachers* (3rd ed.). Harcourt Brace Jovanovich College Publishers.

Goldring, E., Rogers, L. K., & Clark, M. A. (2020). *Leading the change: A comparison of the principal supervisor role in principal supervisor initiative districts and other districts*. Vanderbilt University/Mathematica.

Gomell, A., Hmelo-Silver, C. E., & Šabanović, S. (2022). Co-constructing professional vision: Teacher and researcher learning in co-design. *Cognition and Instruction, 40*(1), 7–26.

Gooden, M. A., & Dantley, M. (2012). Centering race in a framework for leadership preparation. *Journal of Research on Leadership Education, 7*(2), 237–253.

Gooden, M. A., Khalifa, M., Arnold, N. W., Brown, K. D., Meyers, C. V., & Welsh, R. (2023). *A culturally responsive school leadership approach to developing equity-centered principals: Considerations for principal pipelines.* Wallace Foundation.

Gooden, M. A., & O'Doherty, A. (2015). Do you see what I see? Fostering aspiring leaders' racial awareness. *Urban Education, 50*(2), 225–255.

Gosling, J., & Mintzberg, H. (2003). The five minds of a manager. *Harvard Business Review, 81*(11), 54–63.

Grissom, J. A., Egalite, A. J., & Lindsay, C. A. (2021). *How principals affect students and schools: A systematic synthesis of two decades of research.* Wallace Foundation.

Grissom, J. A., Loeb, S., & Masters, B. (2013). Effective instructional time use for school leaders: Longitudinal evidence from observations of principals. *Educational Researcher, 42*(8), 433–444.

Gronn, P. (2002). Distributed leadership as a unit of analysis. *The Leadership Quarterly, 13*(4), 423–451.

Gronn, P. (2003). Leadership: Who needs it? *School Leadership & Management, 23*(3), 267–290.

Grubb, W. N. (2009). *The money myth: School resources, outcomes, and equity.* Russell Sage.

Grubb, W. N., & Flessa, J. J. (2006). "A job too big for one": Multiple principals and other nontraditional approaches to school leadership. *Educational Administration Quarterly, 42*(4), 518–550.

Grubb, W. N., & Lazerson, M. (2004). *The education gospel: The economic goal of schooling.* Harvard University Press.

Grubb, W. N., & Tredway L. (2010). *Leading from the inside out: Expanded roles of teachers in equitable schools.* Paradigm Press.

Guajardo, M., & Guajardo, F. (2013). The power of pláticas. *Reflections, 13*(1), 159–164.

Guajardo, M., Guajardo, F., Janson, C., & Militello, M. (2016). *Reframing community partnerships in education: Uniting the power of place and wisdom of people.* Routledge.

Gutiérrez, K. D. (2016). Designing resilient ecologies: Designing social experiments and a new social imagination. *Educational Researcher, 45*(3), 187–196.

Habermas, J. (1984). *The theory of communicative action: Lifeworld and system world: A critique of functionalist reason* (Vol. 2, T. McCarthy, Trans.). Beacon Press.

Hale, C. R. (2008). *Engaging contradictions: Theory, politics, and methods of activist scholarship.* University of California Press.

Halverson, R., & Halverson, E. (2019). *Education as design for learning: A model for integrating education inquiry across research traditions.* Wisconsin Center for Education Research.

Hammond, Z. (2015). *Culturally responsive teaching and the brain: Promoting authentic engagement and rigor among culturally and linguistically diverse students.* Corwin.

Helig, J. V., Brewer, T. J., & Adamson, F. (2020). The comingling of neoliberal ideology, methods, and funding in school choice politics and research. In M. Berends, A. Primus, & M. G. Springer (Eds.), *Handbook of research on school choice* (pp. 335–350). Routledge.

Herman, L. G. (2013). *Future primal: How our wilderness origins show us the way forward.* New World Library.

Herr, K., & Anderson, G. L. (2014). *The action research dissertation: A guide for students and faculty* (2nd ed.). Sage.

Hochbein, C., Mahone, A., & Vanderbeck, S. (2021). A systematic review of principal time use research. *Journal of Educational Administration*, *59*(2), 215–232.

Hoggan, C., & Militello, M. (2015). Digital stories to promote reflection and community in doctoral education. *Journal of Continuing Higher Education*, *63*(2), 119–125.

Honig, M. I. (2012). District central office leadership as teaching: How central office administrators support principals' development as instructional leaders. *Education Administration Quarterly*, *48*(4), 733–744.

Honig, M. I., & Rainey, L. R. (2020). *Supervising principals for instructional leadership*. Harvard Education Press.

Horn, I. S., & Little, J. W. (2010). Attending to problems of practice: Routines and resources for professional learning in teachers' workplace interactions. *American Education Research Journal*, *47*(1), 181–217.

Hughes, P., & Grace, B. (2011). *Gracious space: A practical guide to working together* (2nd ed.). Center for Ethical Leadership.

hunter, l., Emerald, E., & Martin, G. (2013). *Participatory activist research in the globalised world: Social change through the cultural professions*. Springer.

Irby, D. J. (2020). *Stuck improving: Racial equity and school leadership*. Harvard Education Press.

Ishimaru, A. (2013). From heroes to organizers: Principals and education organizing in urban school reform. *Educational Administration Quarterly*, *49*(1), 3–51.

Jackson, M. (2023). *Uncertain: The wisdom and wonder of being unsure*. Prometheus Books.

Jacobs J., & Casciola, V. (2016). Supervision for social justice. In J. Glanz & S. J. Zepeda (Eds.), *Supervision: New perspectives for theory and practice* (pp. 221–239). Rowman & Littlefield.

Joyful Learning Network. (n.d.). What is joyful learning? http://www.joyfullearningnetwork.com/what-is-joyful-learning.html

Kafka, J. (2009). The principalship in historical perspective. *Peabody Journal of Education*, *84*(3), 318–390.

Kemmis, S., McTaggart, R., & Nixon, R. (2014). *The action research planner: Doing critical participatory action research*. Springer.

Kendi, I. X. (2019). *How to be an anti-racist*. One World.

Khalifa, M. (2018). *Culturally responsive school leadership*. Harvard Education Press.

Khalifa, M., Gooden, M. A., & Davis, J. E. (2016). Culturally responsive school leadership: A synthesis of the literature. *Review of Educational Research*, *86*(4), 1272–1311.

Kim, T., & Mauldin, C. (2022). Troubling unintended harm of heroic discourses in social justice leadership. *Frontiers in Education, 7*(796200), 1–13.

Knowles, M. S. (1980). *The modern practice of adult education: From pedagogy to andragogy*. Cambridge Adult Education.

Ladson-Billings, G. (2014). Culturally relevant pedagogy 2.0: AKA the remix. *Harvard Educational Review, 84*(1), 74–84.

Lambert, L. (2002, May 2002). A framework for shared leadership. *Educational Leadership, 59*(8), 37–40.

Lareau, A. (1989). Family-school relationships: A view from the classsroom. *Educational Policy, 3*(3), 245–259.

Lear, J. (2006). *Radical hope: Ethics in the face of cultural devastation*. Harvard University Press.

Leithwood, K., Harris, A., & Hopkins, D. (2020). Seven strong claims about successful school leadership revisited. *School Leadership & Management, 40*(1), 5–22.

Leithwood, K., & Louis, K. S. (2012). *Linking leadership to student learning*. Jossey-Bass.

Leverett, L. (2002). *Warriors to advance equity: A case for distributing leadership*. The Mid-Atlantic Educational Laboratory.

Levinson, M., Geron, T., & Brighouse, H. (2022). Conceptions of educational equity. *AERA Open, 8*(1), 1–12.

Little, J. W. (1990). The persistence of privacy: Autonomy and initiative in teachers' professional relations. *Teachers College Record, 91*(4), 509–536.

Lortie, D. (1975) *Schoolteacher: A sociological study*. University of Chicago Press.

Love, B. L. (2019). *We want to do more than survive: Abolitionist teaching and the pursuit of educational freedom*. Beacon Press.

Lyman, F. T. (1987). The ThinkTrix: A classroom tool for thinking in response to reading. *Reading: Issues and practices, yearbook of the State of Maryland International Reading Association Council, 4*, 15–18.

Lyman, F. T., Tredway, L., & Purser, M. (2023). Think-pair-share and ThinkTrix: Standard bearers of student dialogue. In R. Gillies, N. A. Davidson, & B. Millis (Eds.), *Contemporary global perspectives on cooperative learning: Applications of CL across educational contexts* (pp. 124–143). Routledge.

Mann, H. (1844). *Secretary's report to the Board of Education of Massachusetts*. Charles C. Little & James Brown. https://ia801305.us.archive.org/27/items/remarksonseventh00asso/remarksonseventh00asso.pdf

March, J. G. (1988). The technology of foolishness. In J. G. March (Ed.), *Decisions and organizations* (pp. 253–265). Basil Blackwell.

March, J. G. (1997). Understanding how decisions happen in organizations. In Z. Shapira (Ed.), *Organizational decision making* (pp. 9–31). Cambridge University Press.

Marris, P. (1974). *Loss and change*. Pantheon Books.

McCullouch, J. (2016). The contributions of teacher confidence to "excellent" mathematical teaching. *Philosophy of Mathematics Education Journal, 30*. https://www.researchgate.net/publication/339645127.

McDonnell, L. M., & Elmore, R. F. (1987). Getting the job done: Alternative policy instruments. *Educational Evaluation and Policy Analysis, 9*(2), 133–152.

McIntyre, D. (2005). Bridging the gap between research and practice. *Cambridge Journal of Education, 33*(3), 357–382.

McKenzie, K. B., & Scheurich, J. J. (2004). Equity traps: A useful construct for preparing principals to lead schools that are successful with racially diverse students. *Education Administration Quarterly, 40*(5), 601–632.

McKoy, D., Eppley, A., & Buss, S. (2022). *Planning cities with young people and schools: Forging justice, generating joy*. Routledge.

Melvin, J. F., Jr. (2017). *Using instructional rounds at the school level to improve classroom instruction*. (Doctoral dissertation, University of California, Berkeley). escholarship.org/uc/item/1ft0s2j4

Merriam, S. B., & Tisdell, E. J. (2015). *Qualitative research: A guide to design and implementation*. John Wiley & Sons.

Mette, I. M., Cormier, D. R., & Oliveras, Y. (2024). *Making a difference: Instructional leadership that drives self-reflection and values the expertise of teachers*. Rowan & Littlefield.

Middlebrooks, A. (2008). Nurturing reflection and connection through the kiva. *Journal of Educational Leadership, 7*(1), 131–139.

Militello, M., & Guajardo, F. (2013). Virtually speaking: How digital storytelling can facilitate organizational learning. *Journal of Community Positive Practices, 13*(2), 80–91.

Militello, M., & Morris, C. (2023). Can I be an equity warrior? *EARCOS Triannual Journal*, Fall, 60–61. https://issuu.com/earcosorg/docs/et-september-2023

Militello, M., Rallis, S. F., & Goldring, E. (2009). *Leading with inquiry and action: How principals improve teaching and learning.* Corwin Press.

Mitchell, R. (2018). *Sacred instructions: Indigenous wisdom for living spirit-based change.* North Atlantic Books.

Morel, R. P., Coburn, C., Catterson, A. K., & Higgs, J. (2019). The multiple meanings of scale: Implications for researcher and practitioners. *Educational Researcher, 48*(6), 369–377.

Nachmanovitch, S. (1991). *Free play: Improvisation in life and art.* G. P. Putnam & Sons.

Nash, J. (2019). *Design thinking in schools: A leader's guide to collaborating for improvement.* Harvard Education Press.

National Academy of Sciences. (2018). *How people learn II: Learners, contexts, and cultures.* The National Academies Press.

National Commission on Excellence. (1983). *A nation at risk.* U.S. Department of Education.

National Institute for Excellence in Teaching (NIET). (2018). *Unleashing teacher leadership: How formal teacher leader roles can improve instruction.* Author.

National Institute for Excellence in Teaching (NIET). (2021). *Untapped potential of the principal supervisor: How support for school leaders should change.* Author.

Norris, J. (2022). *School leaders' sensemaking and sensegiving.* Brill.

O'Day, J. A., & Smith, M. A. (2016). *Equality and quality in U.S. education: Systemic problems, systemic solutions.* American Institute of Research Education Policy Center.

O'Doherty, A., & Ovando, M. N. (2013). Leading learning: First year principals' reflections on instructional leadership. *Journal of School Leadership, 23*(3), 424–581.

Ordoñez-Jasis, R., & Myck-Wayne, J. (2012). Community mapping in action: Uncovering resources and assets for young children and their families. *Young Exceptional Children, 15*(3), 31–45.

Orland-Barak, L., & Maskit, D. (2017). *Methodologies of mediation in professional learning.* Springer.

Palmer, P. J. (1983). *The company of strangers: Christians and the renewal of America's public life.* PublishDrive.

Paris, D., & Alim, H. S. (2017). *Culturally sustaining pedagogies: Teacher and learning for justice in a changing world.* Teachers College Press.

Parker, P. (2018). *The art of gathering: How we meet and why it matters.* Riverhead Books.

Patkin, D., & Greenstein, Y. (2020). Mathematics anxiety and mathematics teaching anxiety of in-service and pre-service primary school teachers. *Teacher Development, 10*(4), 1–18.

Pavlik, R. (2003, July). *The kiva experience.* Cardinal Stritch University Annual Leadership Institute.

Pearson, P. D., Madda, C. I., & Raphael, T. E. (2023). Current issues and best practices in literacy instruction. In L. M. Morrow, E. Morrell, & H. Casey (Eds.), *Best practices in literacy instruction* (7th ed., pp. 3–40). Guilford Press.

Peltier, S. M. (2021), The child is capable: Anishinaabe pedagogy of land and community. *Frontiers in Education, 6*(689445), 1–9.

Petrides, L. A., & Guiney, S. Z. (2002). Knowledge management for school leaders: An ecological framework for thinking schools. *Teachers College Record, 104*(8), 1702–1717.

Piaget, J. (1968). Piaget's point of view. *International Journal of Psychology, 3*(4), 281–299.

Pink, D. (2006). *A whole new mind: Why right-brainers will rule the future.* Riverhead Books.

Principal Leadership Institute. (2010). *Equity-centered professional learning community (ECPLC) professional development program.* Unpublished Report. U.C. Berkeley.

Radd, S., Generett, G. G., Gooden, M. A., & Theoharis, G. (2021). *Five practices for equity-focused school leadership.* Association of Supervision and Curriculum Development.

Resnick, L. B., Asterhan, C. S. C., & Clarke, S. N. (Eds.). (2015). *Socializing intelligence through academic talk and dialogue.* American Education Research Association.

Restoule, J. P. (2017). Where Indigenous knowledge lives: Bringing Indigenous perspectives to online learning environments. In E. A. McKinley & L. T. Smith (Eds.), *Handbook of Indigenous education* (pp. 1295–1317). Springer.

Rigby, J. G., & Tredway, L. (2015). Actions matter: How school leaders enact equity principles. In M. Khalifa, N. A. Witherspoon, A. F. Osanloo, & C. M. Grant (Eds.), *Handbook of urban educational leadership* (pp. 426–440). Rowan & Littlefield.

Roberts, C. (2023). Looking back to find a way forward: Teachings from my ancestors. *Papers on Postsecondary Learning and Teaching, 6*, 49–55.

Robinson, V. M. J., Lloyd, C., & Rowe, K. (2008). The impact of leadership on student outcomes: An analysis of the differential effects of leadership types. *Educational Administration Quarterly, 44*(5), 635–674.

Rogers, E. (2003). *Diffusion of innovation* (5th ed.). Free Press.

Rosa, L., & Toncelli, R. (2022). Avoiding the drive by: Innovative approaches to professional development. *Academia Letters,* Article 5787. https://doi.org/10.20935/AL578

Rost, J. C. (1991). *Leadership for the twenty-first century.* Praeger.

Rowan, B. (1990). Commitment and control: Alternative strategies for the organizational design of schools. In C. B. Cazden (Ed.), *Review of research in education* (Vol. 16, pp. 353–389). American Educational Research Association.

Safir, S., & Dugan, J. (2021). *Street data: A next-generation model for equity, pedagogy, and school transformation.* Jossey-Bass.

Saldaña, J. (2016). *The coding manual for qualitative researchers.* Sage.

Saphier, J. (1993). *How to make supervision and evaluation really work: Supervision and evaluation in the context of strengthening school culture.* Research for Better Teaching.

Schneider, J., & Berkshire, J. (2020). *The wolf at the schoolhouse door.* The New Press.

Schön, D. (1973). *Beyond the stable state: Public and private learning in a changing society.* Norton.

Schön, D. (1987). *Educating the reflective practitioner.* Jossey-Bass.

Scott, J. T. (2016). The politics of market-based education reform. In W. J. Matthis & T. M. Trujillo (Eds.), *Learning from the federal market-based reforms: Lessons from ESSA* (pp. 9–36). Information Age Publishing.

Sebastian, J., & Allensworth, E. (2019). Linking leadership to organizational growth and student achievement: A modertation mediation analysis. *Teachers College Record, 121*(9), 1–32.

Sebastian, J., Allensworth, E., & Stevens, D. (2014). The influence of school leadership on classroom participation: Examining configurations of organizational supports. *Teachers College Record, 116*(8), 1–36.

Sergiovanni, T. J. (2000). *The lifeworld of leadership: Creating culture, community, and personal meaning in our schools*. Jossey Bass.

Sharatt, L. D., & Fullan, M. (2022). *Putting FACES on the data: What great leaders and teachers do*. Corwin.

Simon, K., Hodgkins, L., & Argent, J. (2021). Small chunks, deep learning: Micro-credentials for equity-driven instructional leadership. In Y. Huang (Ed.), *Handbook of research on credential innovations for inclusive pathways to professions* (pp. 276–299). IGI Global.

Singleton, G. (2015). *Courageous conversations about race: A field guide to achieving equity in schools* (2nd ed.). Corwin.

Smith, M. S., & Stein, M. K. (2011). *5 practices for orchestrating productive math discussions*. National Council of Teachers of Mathematics.

Snowden, D. J., & Boone, M. E. (2007). A leader's framework for decision making. *Harvard Business Review, 85*(11), 68–76.

Spillane, J. (2006). *Distributed leadership*. Jossey-Bass.

Spillane, J. P. (2013). Diagnosing and designing for schoolhouse practice. In H. J. Malone (Ed.), *Leading educational change: Global issues, challenges, and lessons on whole-system reform* (pp. 37–41). Teachers College Press.

Spillane, J. P., & Coldren, A. F. (2011). *Diagnosis and design for school improvement*. Teachers College Press.

Spillane, J. P., Halverson, R., & Diamond, J. B. (2001). Investigating school leadership practice: A distributed perspective. *Educational Researcher, 30*(3), 23–28.

Stahl, R. J. (1990). *Using "think-time" and "wait-time" skillfully in the classroom*. ERIC Clearinghouse for Social Studies/Social Science Education.

Steele, C. (2010). *Whistling Vivaldi: And other clues to how stereotypes affect us*. W. W. Norton.

Stein, M. K., Engle, R. A., Smith, M. A., & Hughes, E. K. (2015). Orchestrating productive mathematical discussions: Helping teachers learn to better incorporate student thinking. In L. B. Resnick, C. S. C. Asterhan, & S. N. Clarke (Eds.), *Socializing intelligence through academic talk and dialogue* (pp. 375–388). American Education Research Association.

Suarez, C. (2018). *The power manual: How to master complex power dynamics*. The New Society Publishers.

Suina, M. (2016). Reflections of a Pueblo Indian health educator. *Journal of American Indian Education, 55*(3), 72–90.

Sullivan, S., & Glanz, J. (2013). *Supervision that improves teaching and learning: Strategies & techniques* (4th ed.). Corwin.

Sutton, S. S., & Gong, N. (2021). Rethinking the "superhero" principal narrative. *Educational Leadership*, *78*(7), 38–43.

Taylor, F. W. (1911). *The principles of scientific management*. Harper.

Theoharis, G. (2024). *The school leaders our children deserve: Seven keys to equity, social justice and school reform* (2nd ed.). Teachers College Press.

Tindle, K., Leconte, P., Buchanan, L., & Taymans, J. (2005, April). Transition planning: Community mapping as a tool for teachers and students. *Research to Practice Brief, 4*(1). National Center on Secondary Education and Transition.

Tredway, L. (1999). The art of juggling: Preparing preservice teachers for urban education. *The Journal of Negro Education, 68*(3), 382–396.

Tredway, L. (2003). *Community mapping: A rationale.* Unpublished manuscript prepared for the Principal Leadership Institute, University of California, Berkeley.

Tredway, L. (2006). *Types of paraphrasing and question stems useful for coaching.* Unpublished.

Tredway, L., & Generett, G. G. (2015). Community story-mapping guide: The pedagogy of the griot. Institute for Educational Leadership. https://iel.org/wp-content/uploads/2015/04/Community_Story-Mapping_Guide-2015-04.pdf)

Tredway, L., Simon, K., Militello, M., Hodgkins, L., & Morris, C. (2019a). *Project I^4 framework of classroom learning and practice: Propelled by equity-driven tools for school change.* East Carolina University. https://education.ecu.edu/projecti4/framework/

Tredway, L., Militello, M., Simon, K., Hodgkins, L., Argent, J., & Morris, C. (2019b). *Tools for equitable observations.* East Carolina University.

Tredway, L., Militello, M., Simon, K., Hodgkins, L., Argent, J., & Morris, C. (2019c). *Effective conversation guide.* East Carolina University. https://education.ecu.edu/wp-content/pv-uploads/sites/171/2019/01/Effective-Conversation-Guide_Project-I4_NOV2020_FINAL-1.pdf

Tredway, L., Argent, J., & Militello, M. (2020). Self-care for school leaders starts now. *ASCD Express: Ready for Restart: Teaching Smarter, 15*(23). https://www.ascd.org/el/articles/self-care-for-school-leaders-starts-now

Tredway, L., Militello, M., & Simon, K. (2021). Making classroom observations matter. *Educational Leadership, 78*(7), 56–62.

Tredway, L., & Militello, M. (2024). Supervision redux: Leaders with teachers activate culturally responsive practices. In D. R. Cormier, I. Mette, & Y.O. Ortiz (Eds.), *Culturally responsive instructional supervision: Instructional leadership for equitable and emancipatory outcomes* (pp. 249–272). Teachers College Press.

Tschannen-Moran, M. (2014). The interconnectivity of trust in schools. In D. Van Maele, P. B. Forsyth, & M. Van Houtte, (Eds.), *Trust and school life: The influence of trust on learning, teaching, leading, and bridging* (pp. 57–81). Springer.

Tschannen-Moran, M., & Hoy, W. K. (2000). The multidisciplinary analysis of the nature, meaning, and measurement of trust. *Review of Educational Research, 70*(4), 547–593.

Tyack, D., & Cuban, L. (1997). *Tinkering toward utopia.* Harvard University Press.

Valencia, R. R. (2010). *Dismantling contemporary deficit thinking: Educational thought and practice.* Routledge.

Valli, L., & Buese, D. (2007). The changing roles of teachers in an era of high-stakes accountability. *American Educational Research Journal, 44*(3), 519–558.

Vygotsky, L. S. (1978). *Mind in society: The development of higher psychological processes.* Harvard University Press.

Wang, C., Yuan, Y., & Feng, M. (1996). Photovoice as a tool for participatory evaluation: The community's view of process and impact. *Journal of Contemporary Health, 4*(3), 7–49.

Wang, F. (2021). Principals' self- and interpersonal leadership amid work intensification. *Journal of School Leadership, 31*(5), 396–427.

Wang, Y. (2020). What is the role of emotions in educational leaders' decision making? Proposing an organizing framework. *Educational Policy Studies Faculty Publications, 41.* https://scholarworks.gsu.edu/eps_facpub/41

Ware, F. (2006). Warm demander pedagogy: Culturally responsive teaching that supports a culture of achievement for African American students. *Urban Education, 41*(4), 427–445.

Weiner, B. (1986). *An attributional theory of motivation and emotion.* Springer.

Weiss, L. (1995). The four "I's" of school reform: How interests, ideology, information, and institutions affect teachers and principals. *Harvard Educational Review, 65*(4), 571–592.

Wenger, E. (1998). Communities of practice: Learning as a social system. *Systems Thinker, 9*(5), 1–10.

Wetzel, M. M., Holyoke, E., Alexander, K. H., Dunham, H., & Collins, C. (2023). *Coaching communities: Pursuing justice, teacher learning, and transformation.* Harvard Education Press.

Wise, D., & Jacobo, A. (2010). Towards a framework for leadership coaching. *School Leadership and Management, 30*(2), 159–169.

Wong, C. -C., Kumpulainen, K., & Kahamaa, A. (2020). Collaborative creativity among education professionals in a co-design workshop: A multidimensional analysis. *Thinking Skills and Creativity, 42*(100971), 1–17.

Woo, L. J., & Henriksen, D. (2023). The critical role of teachers in educational design processes. *Teachers College Record.* Commentary. https://journals.sagepub.com/page/tcz/collections/commentaries

Woodson, C. G. (1933). *The miseducation of the Negro.* Africa World Press.

Woulfin, S. L., Stevenson, I., & Lord, K. (2023). *Making coaching matter: Leading continuous improvement in schools.* Teachers College Press.

Woulfin, S. L., & Weiner, J. (2017). Triggering change: An investigation of the logics of turnaround. *Education and Urban Society, 51*(2), 222–246.

Xenofontes, C., & Andrews, P. (2023). The experiential construction of mathematics teacher identity and the impact of early mathematical failure. *Frontiers in Education,* 8 (1158973). https://doi.org/10.3389/feduc.2023.1158973

Yosso, T. J. (2005). Whose culture has capital? A critical race theory discussion of community cultural wealth. *Race, Ethnicity and Education, 8*(1), 69–91.

Yurkofsky, M. M., Petersen, M. J., Mehta, J. D., Horwitz-Willis, R., & Frumin, K. M. (2020). Research on continuous improvement: Exploring the complexities of managing educational change. *Review of Research in Education, 44*(1), 403–433.

Zepeda, S. (2016). *Instructional supervision: Applying tools and concepts* (4th ed.). Routledge.

Zepeda, S. J. (2007). *Instructional supervision: Applying tools and concepts.* Eye of Education.

Zwiers, J., & Crawford, M. (2011). *Academic conversations: Classroom talk that fosters critical thinking and classroom understanding.* Stenhouse.

DISSERTATION REFERENCES

All dissertations are available through East Carolina University Joyner Library website. https://library.ecu.edu/

Abdolcader, F. (2023). *Using equitable pedagogy to support English language learners in academic conversations* [Doctoral dissertation, East Carolina University].

Ahmad, Z. (2023). *Black students matter: How teachers equitably engage African American students in understanding conceptual mathematics* [Doctoral dissertation, East Carolina University].

Britt, L. (2023). *Creating a home: Promoting equitable academic discourse by establishing teacher agency and co-design* [Doctoral dissertation, East Carolina University].

Caruz, V. (2023). *Kapwa (shared identity): Filipino American perspectives and responses to educational leadership* [Doctoral dissertation, East Carolina University].

Collins, L. (2023). *The sweet spot of mentoring minds and building support* [Doctoral dissertation, East Carolina University].

Cooper, R. (2023). *Language is not my hurdle: Improving equitable instructional practices for English language learners one classroom at a time* [Doctoral dissertation, East Carolina University].

Cruthis, C. (2024). *Tacit leadership: Orchestrating teacher leadership to develop a peer coaching program for inquiry-based instructional practices* [Doctoral dissertation, East Carolina University].

Dupree, L. (2023). *Repositioning our thinking: Using culturally responsive practices to increase equitable access to rigorous instruction* [Doctoral dissertation, East Carolina University].

Edwards, D. (2023). *Cultivating equity warriors: Empowering educators to enact responsive pedagogy for African American students* [Doctoral dissertation, East Carolina University].

Garcia, M. (2021). *Social justice warriors: Coaching teachers to develop culturally responsive pedagogy* [Doctoral dissertation, East Carolina University].

Geathers, C. (2023). *Getting into good trouble: Building culturally responsive teacher practices for African American student success in mathematics* [Doctoral dissertation, East Carolina University].

James, J. (2023). *Leave this place better than you found it: Facilitating inquiry-based learning experiences* [Doctoral dissertation, East Carolina University].

Kasner, M. (2023). *Joyful learning matters: Teacher practices in amplifying joyful learning experiences for Chinese English language learners* [Doctoral dissertation, East Carolina University].

Koh, P. (2023). *Finding leadership 정 (belonging): A critical race ethnography of Asian American leadership* [Doctoral dissertation, East Carolina University].

Lappé, G. (2023). *They're speaking: Gender identity, agency, and belonging in an international middle school* [Doctoral dissertation, East Carolina University].

Lassiter, J. (2023). *The missing piece to teacher induction: A framework for adding equity-focused support to induction* [Doctoral dissertation, East Carolina University].

Lau-Yee, D. (2023). *Leap for joy: Amplifying joyful learning outcomes for Chinese ELL students* [Doctoral dissertation, East Carolina University].

Ledo-Lane, A. (2023). *Using creative practices to foster arts integration: Supporting experiential pedagogy for teachers* [Doctoral dissertation, East Carolina University].

Machado, M. (2021). *Family stories matter: Critical pedagogy of storytelling in fifth-grade classroom* [Doctoral dissertation, East Carolina University].

McDuffie, N. (2023). *Equitable classrooms require equitable practices: How do teachers develop and implement culturally responsive teaching in support of equitable classrooms* [Doctoral dissertation, East Carolina University].

Moon, M. (2023). *Islands of innovation: Examining the nexus between culturally responsive relationships and cognitively demanding academic discourse* [Doctoral dissertation, East Carolina University].

Morris, C. (2023). *White women educational leaders: Embodying antiracism in eastern North Carolina* [Doctoral dissertation, East Carolina University].

Mudd, T. (2023). *Butts, books, buses, and better instruction: How a principal can develop assistant principals into equity-centered instructional leaders by juggling tasks together* [Doctoral dissertation, East Carolina University].

Palmer, M. (2021). *Connecting the dots: The intersection of teacher readiness and principal actions* [Doctoral dissertation, East Carolina University].

Parker, J. (2023). *Collaborative spaces for leaders: A participatory action research study to improve district and school leader collaboration* [Doctoral dissertation, East Carolina University].

Payne, B. (2023). *Experiential conditions for educational equity in action: Culturally responsive leadership development in an international school* [Doctoral dissertation, East Carolina University].

Purser, P. (2019). *Pump up the volume: Amplifying student dialogue in 21st century ELL classrooms* [Doctoral dissertation, East Carolina University].

Quadros-Meis, M. (2021). *Cultivating brave space: How networks fortify school leaders to ensure equitable outcomes for Black youth* [Doctoral dissertation, East Carolina University].

Rosenthal, L. (2019). *Fits and starts: One elementary school's journey toward trauma-informed leadership* [Doctoral dissertation, East Carolina University].

Scott, H. (2023). *Filling the void: Building and sustaining cohesive and consistent instructional leadership* [Doctoral dissertation, East Carolina University].

Tang, W. (2023). *Equity warriors: Building principal capacity to enact culturally responsive leadership* [Doctoral dissertation, East Carolina University].

Triplett, M. (2019). *Talk smart: A participatory action research project implementing academic discourse in an urban middle school* [Doctoral dissertation, East Carolina University].

Velasco, C. (2021). *Espacio sano: How social justice educational leaders cultivate caring and sharing* [Doctoral dissertation, East Carolina University].

Index

About the Authors

Lynda Tredway is the program coordinator for East Carolina University (ECU) International EdD and was the project coordinator for USDOE-funded Project I^4 at the Institute for Educational Leadership, a partner of ECU, to design and implement microcredentials for school leaders. Previously, she was the founding director of the Principal Leadership Institute at University of California, Berkeley (2000–2012); she coordinated a teacher residency program at George Washington University and was a public school teacher and coordinator in District of Columbia public schools. She co-authored a book on teacher leadership, *Leading from the Inside Out: Expanded Roles for Teachers in Equitable Schools.* Recent publications include practice-based articles in *Educational Leadership* and research articles in peer-reviewed journals on the international doctorate and Project I^4 results, all of which are co-authored with Matt Militello and Project I^4 team members. Lynda is a mother and grandmother living in Washington, D.C. She is working on a multi-quilt project entitled "The Lynching Trees: Leaves of Redemption for America" that represents persons who were lynched in the United States.

Matthew Militello is the Wells Fargo Distinguished Professor in educational leadership at East Carolina University. He has held faculty positions at North Carolina State University and the University of Massachusetts at Amherst. Prior to his academic career, Militello was a middle and high public school teacher, assistant principal, and principal in Michigan. Militello has more than 60 publications, including six books. Militello has received more than $23 million in external funding. Militello is the founding director of an executive EdD program hosted each summer in Bangkok, Thailand. In 2023, he was awarded the ECU Eminent Career Trend Setter Award. He earned his undergraduate teaching degree from the University of Michigan and his masters and PhD in educational administration from Michigan State University. Matt has been married to Elizabeth for 30 years and is the father of four wonderful boys.

Joseph Flessa is professor of educational leadership and policy and the associate dean of programs at the Ontario Institute for Studies in Education of the University of Toronto. Before earning his PhD at the University of California, Berkeley, he was a public school teacher in Texas and director of an international school in Mexico. His scholarship focuses on urban educational policy and politics, comparative educational administration, and school leadership and policy with an emphasis on leadership practices in Ontario and Latin American schools. At OISE he helped develop the First Nations Schools Principals' Course, is core faculty of the Centre for Leadership and Diversity, and is widely regarded as an exemplary teacher and dedicated supervisor. In 2021, he was awarded OISE's *Distinguished Contributions to Teaching Award.*